Birding

IN ATLANTIC CANADA

Birding

IN ATLANTIC CANADA

NOVA SCOTIA

Roger Burrows

JESPERSON PRESS LTD.

Jesperson Press Ltd.
39 James Lane
St. John's, Newfoundland
A1E 3H3

Cover and text design: Jesperson Press Ltd., St. John's, NF
Cover illustration: Robert Villani, Kew Gardens, N.Y.
Typesetting, Printing and Binding: Jesperson Printing Limited, St. John's, NF

Appreciation is expressed to *The Canada Council* for its assistance in publishing this book.

The publisher acknowledges the financial contribution of the *Cultural Affairs Division* of the *Department of Culture, Recreation and Youth, Government of Newfoundland and Labrador* which has helped make this publication possible.

Canadian Cataloguing in Publication Data

Burrows, Roger, 1942-

Birding in Atlantic Canada

Includes index.
Bibliography: p.
Partial contents: v.1. Nova Scotia
ISBN 0-920502-87-3 (set)
ISBN 0-920502-89-X (v. 1)

1. Bird watching — Atlantic Provinces.
2. Birds — Atlantic Provinces
— Geographical distribution.   3. Bird
watching — Nova Scotia — Geographical
distribution.   I. Title
QL685.5.A8B87 1988   598.29715   C88-098644-1

Acknowledgements

by Roger Burrows

A chance encounter, at the age of 11, with a common, but highly colorful, male Chaffinch on a friend's lawn in England literally changed my life. A pair of X3 opera glasses may have been a poor excuse for field glasses, but they succeeded in opening my eyes to the natural world. I wasn't alone, as my twin brother, Tony, also got bitten by the bird-watching bug.

At the same time, older schoolmates started a field club which ranged farther afield until we finally reached, a full year later, the Mecca of birding at the time — Cley, Norfolk. Richard Richardson was guide to our group on several occasions and we couldn't have asked for a better teacher. Richard died just over 10 years ago, but I can still remember his incredible knowledge and sense of fun. My spark was ignited as quickly as that on Richard's 750 cc Triumph, and I am eternally grateful for the inspiration he provided. This book is a tribute to him and those hours on East Bank.

I can't take all the credit for this book as much of it is based on information provided in questionnaires sent around in 1979 and from articles and reports published in Nova Scotia Birds. There are many birding sites I have yet to visit, but I am gradually cutting down the number and eventually hope to check out every site mentioned in this book. Anyone mentioned in the text as a contact has provided information, and I would like to take this opportunity to thank each of them for sharing birding knowledge.

Last, but certainly not least, I must thank my long-suffering daughter, Sharon, who has endured the vagrancy of a father who spends much of his leisure time chasing after "some bird or another". This has meant taking messages over the phone, spending more time than usual on the road, and even freezing on a few Christmas Bird Counts. Believe me, Sharon, some day you'll say it's all been worth it!

Dedication

This book is dedicated to my mother, Edith Frances, whose drawing skills are inherited by a far less accomplished artist, and to my late father, Thomas, who instilled in me a love of travel. Both traits have been invaluable in my chosen obsession.

Table of Contents

Preface

by Blake Maybank

It was a bit of a shock when I, a person born and raised on the prairies of Canada, moved east, especially when my new job took me to an isolated community on the west coast of Newfoundland. And since my hobby was birding, the anxiety increased. Everything was new, and fellow birders seemed as rare as Snow Buntings in July. What species could I expect to encounter, and where and when should I go to look for them? It was then that I met Roger Burrows. It was a fortuitous moment.

As a birder, Roger was more fanatic even than I (however vehemently he denied it), and he delighted in both discovering new birding areas and re-exploring old ones. Thereafter, I seldom ventured out without his *Birdwatcher's Guide to Atlantic Canada* at hand. It variously guided, cajoled, suggested and predicted, and it made some mistakes as well, for it was breaking new ground. Volume 1 of the guide (the only one published) was a bold effort, covering an enormous amount of territory, including a few locales where no birder, including Roger, had gone before. But he was not too shy to make predictions, and he was very successful at enticing me to visit places known and unknown throughout the province of Newfoundland. And it was more than a birding guide — it gave a sense of spirit and warmth to each headland and harbour, from Mummichog to Joe Batt's Arm, from Chance Cove to Ha Ha Bay. With Roger's advice, I explored and discovered, and in time helped to increase the knowledge of the birdlife of easternmost North America.

In the years since my arrival, Roger and I have birded together often, and memorable events have accumulated like swallows on a wire: Common Ringed Plover at Glovertown; six Christmas Bird Counts in seven days; Buff-breasted Sandpipers at two metres range; being the first to see 100 species in a day in Newfoundland. I am grateful for these experiences, and for the assistance Roger has given myself and others birding in Newfoundland.

Roger's new birding book is a timely arrival, for I have just moved to Nova Scotia and am again in need of help and inspiration. I will use his book often, as should you. There is much to discover in its pages, as there is in this beautiful province. Explore, enjoy and learn.

Sites profiled in this guide

Mainland Nova Scotia

1 Yarmouth Area	8 Wolfville Area
2 Seal Island	9 Halifax — Dartmouth
3 Cape Sable	10 The Circuit
4 Matthews Lake	11 Cobequid Bay
5 Lunenburg County	12 Amherst Point
6 Kejimkujik	13 Northumberland Strait
7 Brier Island	14 Antigonish Area

Cape Breton & Sable Island

15 Cheticamp Area
16 Ingonish Area
17 Bird Islands
18 Glace Bay Sanctuary
19 Louisbourg Area
20 Sable Island

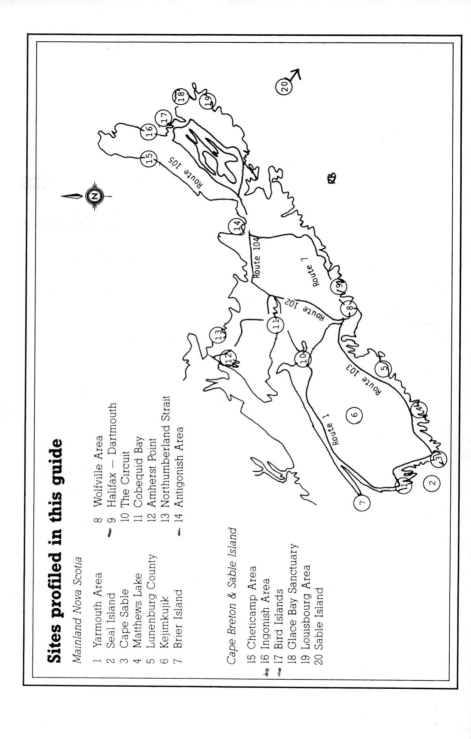

Introduction

Nova Scotia is one of the oldest settled regions in North America and one of the more picturesque. The scenery is varied from mountains in Cape Breton to farmlands in the Annapolis Valley. Resource-based industries such as fishing, farming and forestry are locally important, although there are manufacturing industries in some towns. Coal-mining was formerly a major activity in Cumberland County and Cape Breton, but only one active mine now remains. Other mining activities are very local. The fastest-growing industry, as in much of Atlantic Canada, is tourism. Hotel and motel accommodation is widespread and there are a number of bed and breakfast establishments, particularly in Cape Breton. Tourism facilities have been improving in the last decade, and the improvements have now been extended to transportation, although budget cutbacks have reduced some services.

The Ocean Playground of Nova Scotia can be reached by car ferry from Maine, New Brunswick, Prince Edward Island and Newfoundland, and by road from New Brunswick. There are also air connections with New Brunswick, Prince Edward Island, Newfoundland, and all parts of the continent from Halifax. Most visitors arrive by the Gulf of Maine car ferries from Portland and Bar Harbour in Maine or the Trans Canada Highway route via Amherst. The Nova Scotia Department of Tourism has tourist information centres at the major access points of Yarmouth, Amherst and Halifax International Airport. There are also tourist information bureaus at North Sydney, Port Hastings, Pictou, Digby and downtown Halifax, while many communities run their own tourist information offices during the summer months.

The Gulf of Maine ferries operate year round and offer a choice of sailing times. The Portland-Yarmouth ferry operated by Prince of Fundy Cruises offers an overnight trip to Yarmouth with return runs during the day. Information can be obtained from the terminal in Portland, Maine and from the Yarmouth terminal. The same route is followed by the Marine Atlantic ferry which leaves Monday, Wednesday and Friday nights from Maine, and Sunday, Tuesday and Thursday afternoons from Nova Scotia. A better route for birders is Marine Atlantic's shorter route from Bar Harbour to Yarmouth. Trips both ways operate during daylight hours and are very productive for birders. Ferries also operate between North Sydney and Argentia and Port aux Basques in Newfoundland, Digby and Saint John, New Brunswick, and Caribou and Wood Islands, Prince Edward Island.

International flights make scheduled stops at Halifax International Airport, and there are daily flights to and from other parts of Atlantic Canada and both Montreal and Toronto. Air Canada and Canadian Airlines International provide long distance services, while Air Nova and Air Atlantic provide connecting flights within the region. Passenger rail service has been downgraded throughout the region, but there are connections with Sydney and the Annapolis Valley from Halifax and Moncton, New Brunswick. Acadian Lines provides the bulk of provincial bus services from their terminal in downtown Halifax. There are routes within the province to Amherst, Sydney, Yarmouth, and connections to New Brunswick and Prince Edward Island.

Of all the Canadian provinces, none is better covered by and for birders per capita than Nova Scotia. As an example of the interest in birds and other aspects of natural history, the Nova Scotia Bird Society and the provincial government co-operated in producing a natural history map of the province which is extremely helpful in planning trips. I don't know how available the map is, but I would recommend it as a necessary travelling companion to supplement this book.

Another useful source of information is the excellent magazine that appears three times a year. Almost every corner of the province has one or two resident birdwatchers who provide regular information for *Nova Scotia Birds*. This helps to keep the Nova Scotia Society's magazine the most highly rated provincial birding periodical in Canada, both for the completeness of its reports and the diversity of its articles. The variety of species and sheer numbers of shorebirds in fall are the envy of birders from the interior, and the magazine is a true reflection of what the province has to offer.

Much of the basic data, and the original impetus, for this book has been gleaned from between the covers of my copies of 16 years of newsletters, which explains why I can write with apparent authority on places I have never visited or last visited ten years ago. I should add that the network of dedicated birdwatchers and birders in the province also supplied information for use in my original volume of *A Birdwatcher's Guide to Atlantic Canada* dealing with Nova Scotia, which was not published due to lack of funds. I hope this publication seven years later will repay them for their help, albeit tardy.

YARMOUTH

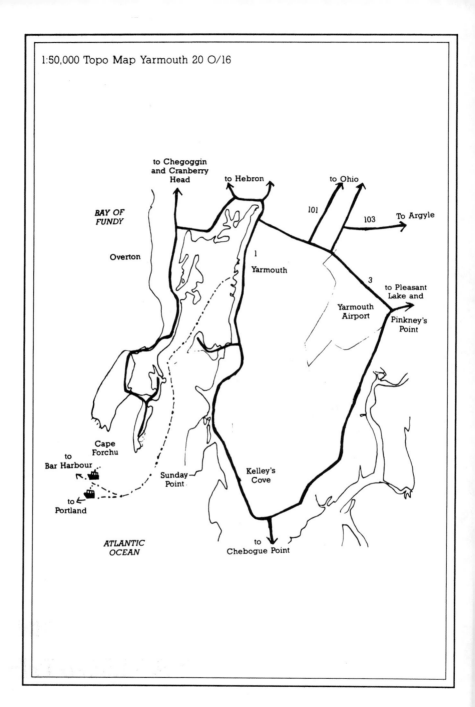

1:50,000 Topo Map Yarmouth 20 O/16

The geographical position of Yarmouth County partly explains why this is one of the best places in Atlantic Canada to study migration in both spring and fall. The long headlands pointing into the Atlantic Ocean are extended even further by numerous islands where exhausted migrants can make a first landfall in spring, and southbound flocks can stage in fall. A second reason is the existence of shallow protected bays between the points where waterfowl and marshbirds can gather and feed. Almost any coastal area at the southwest tip of Nova Scotia rates a visit at any time of year.

This area has been very well covered by members of the Nova Scotia Bird Society who wrote about it and eventually expanded their information into "Where to Find the Birds in Nova Scotia". Because I have made only one visit, and a very brief one at that, I have used their information and supplemented it with records and information from "Nova Scotia Birds", including area guides. I have chosen the Yarmouth area as the site because it is handy to the ferry, but I suspect the whole county deserves to be visited.

Yarmouth itself is a small town dating back to 1761 when three families arrived from Massachusetts, soon to be joined by several Acadian families and about 20 years later by many Loyalist families. It retains its timeless air with its long waterfront, lawns, gardens and shade trees, all receiving a fair share of birds throughout the year. Spring arrives early, although a mid February **Longeared Owl** undoubtedly jumped the gun. More likely early migrants are **Snowy and Great Egrets** on the mudflats in early April when the birds offshore include good numbers of northbound **Northern Gannet**, seaducks, gulls and terns. There has even been a **Parasitic Jaeger** venturing close to town in mid-month, and **Mute Swan and Lesser Golden Plover** later on.

The town's shade trees regularly attract **Scarlet Tanager, Northern Oriole and Indigo Bunting** in spring, and there have been fairly frequent stopovers by **Warbling Vireo, Summer Tanager, Orchard Oriole, Blue Grosbeak and House Finch** in recent years. There are often **Northern Oriole** nests in summer, but the most famous breeding birds are the pairs of **Northern Cardinal** that have chosen to stay here more than any other community in Atlantic Canada. One of the most unusual summer visitors was an early July **Scissortailed Flycatcher**. The short walk to the lighthouse can be very rewarding from mid July, when the first shorebirds trickle in. The harbour is always a good place to see gulls year-round and watch parties of **Doublecrested Cormorant and Great Blue Heron** among the massed shorebirds. **Little Blue Heron** is a possibility any time in spring and summer, and so is **Snowy Egret**. I missed it on my only summer trip on the "Bluenose", but Yarmouth harbour is also a good place to test your powers of observation and identification in an effort to find a **Roseate Tern** among the **Common and Arctic Terns** at its entrance.

By early August the numbers of shorebirds, especially **Shortbilled Dowitcher and Semipalmated Sandpiper**, have increased and some flocks start to move to outlying areas. Fall is certainly an excellent time to visit Yarmouth, late September-early December period providing most of the rarities. **Roseate Tern, Buffbreasted Sandpiper and Sabine's Gull** have all appeared in August when the numbers of songbirds are a little lower.

Almost every species migrating through Nova Scotia has turned up here at one time or another in fall. Waterbirds are not a major attraction, although **American Coot and Laughing Gull** rate a mention. Much more noticeable in the peak migration period are the landbirds — everything from **Yellowbilled Cuckoo and Great Crested Flycatcher** to **Blue Grosbeak and Rufous-sided Towhee. Nashville and Pine Warblers, Summer Tanager, Dickcissel, Indigo Bunting and Whitecrowned Sparrow** are all regular at this time, and the number of **Blue Grosbeaks**, previously a spring visitor only, is increasing. Other notable migrants have included **Varied Thrush and Bluegray Gnatcatcher**. The warm climate and overcast days lull many songbirds into a false sense of security, which explains the overwintering of **Brown Thrasher, Hermit Thrush, Yellowbreasted Chat, Rusty Blackbird and Rufous-sided Towhee** with the resident **Northern Cardinals**. The most unexpected early winter visitors were, however, not songbirds (at least not in the accepted sense!) — **Tundra Swans** have made two whistle-stops in late November. Other waterfowl seen in Yarmouth harbour in winter include **Northern Pintail and Lesser Scaup**.

Just north of Yarmouth are some headlands that offer an unobstructed view of the approach to the Bay of Fundy. The best approach is north past the fountain and hospital on Leif Erikson Drive, where the pond has attracted **Gadwall and Roughwinged Swallow** in spring, towards Overton. Make the left turn here on Yarmouth Bar to Markland and you end up at Cape Forchu. This is an excellent area for a seawatch and a **Doublecrested Cormorant** made a nice first bird of the year on New Year's Day one year. Spring is the time to watch for **Northern Gannet** and stormblown inshore **Leach's Storm-petrel, Red and Rednecked Phalaropes. Harlequin** are irregular winter residents and spring migrants, but the most compelling birds are the marshbirds. **Great and Snowy Egrets** are to be expected, but a late May **White Ibis** would have to be considered brighter than white.

Greater and Sooty Shearwaters wheel by in summer when **Manx Shearwater** is also a possibility, and the recent reports of **South Polar Skua** in the Bay of Fundy suggest that any **Great Skua** warrants a second look. Cape Forchu is a good place to look for shorebirds after mid July, especially **Willet and Shortbilled Dowitcher**, with the **Least and Semipalmated Sandpipers** often put to flight by a **Great, Snowy or Cattle Egret**, all of which are regular here in late summer. The coastal fringe can also be searched for rarer songbirds such as **Marsh Wren, Philadelphia Vireo, Bluewinged Warbler, Grasshopper and Vesper Sparrows** from mid August on.

A return to town can be made by way of Cranberry Head which offers another chance to look for seabirds. These have included **Great Skua, Laughing Gull and Caspian**

Tern in recent years. **Great and Snowy Egrets** are also regular temporary residents in spring and fall. A **Redshouldered Hawk** was an unusual visitor, and so were **Prothonotary Warbler and Western Tanager** — both very rare visitors to the mainland part of the province.

Just south of Yarmouth is Sunday Point. This is good any day of the week, especially in fall when the shorebirds take it over. About 12 species are normal with **200 Semipalmated Plover and 400 Semipalmated Sandpiper** the commonest birds. **Killdeer and Piping Plover** are also to be found among the small parties of **Willet, Greater Yellowlegs, Shortbilled Dowitcher, Least Sandpiper and Sanderling**. A search will also turn up **Blackbellied Plover, Ruddy Turnstone, Dunlin, Solitary, Pectoral and Baird's Sandpipers**.

About 2 miles south of town is another interesting headland reached by following a narrow track from Kelley's Cove to the right over a hill and then down to a small sandy beach backed by a tidal marsh. Shorebirds are plentiful here and there is a small summer population of **Sharptailed Sparrow**. Another 3 miles on, a pebble ridge indicates Chebogue Point with ample parking for a walk to a drumlin leading east along the ridge. A winter visit to the point itself will reveal some **Horned Lark and Snow Bunting** parties and may turn up a few **Water Pipits** left over from the large flocks of fall when totals of 150 are not unusual. The vegetable fields are the places to look for blackbirds and sparrows, which often include a few **Whitecrowned Sparrows**.

Blackbellied Plover pay a brief visit in spring, and the most obvious summer residents are **Barn, Cliff and Bank Swallows** overhead, and **Bobolink, Song and Savannah Sparrows** in the grasses. **Redheaded Woodpecker and Northern Cardinal** were obviously on their way to other habitats. Shorebirds are best seen in the fall. Numbers are not high, but the fields attract **Lesser Golden and Blackbellied Plovers, and Buffbreasted Sandpiper** and the occasional **Upland Sandpiper**. There are also large flocks of **Shortbilled Dowitcher** on the marshes and **Lesser Yellowlegs and Red Knot** on the gravel spit fringing the lower salt marsh. **Ringbilled Gull** parties can build up in late fall when an **American Coot** was an unusual visitor.

Herons and Egrets

This area is very popular with migrants, especially landbirds which use it as a last land base before heading south. **Northern Harrier, Merlin and American Kestrel** can be found heading out to sea here, and another group using it in this way are the flycatchers. Large numbers of **Eastern Kingbird** move down the point from late August to early September, and they have been joined by occasional **Western Kingbirds** and even a **Scissortailed Flycatcher**. Songbirds also leave by this method with warblers and sparrows particularly common later on. **Sharptailed Sparrow** nests here and is commonly seen on migration with flocks of **Savannah Sparrow**. Even forest species like **Redbreasted Nuthatch and Rubycrowned Kinglet** use the mainly agricultural land as a stepping-off point. Late in the fall straggling **Northern Harrier and American Kestrel** check for late migrants, and an occasional **Roughlegged Hawk or Shorteared Owl** can be found quartering the pastures for a hapless rodent.

Other places to visit from this site

Just north of Yarmouth and reached by taking the Highway 340 turnoff at Pleasant Lake are the attractive woods and waters of Ellenwood Park. **Common Loon** are relatively common breeding birds and a pair of **Hooded Merganser** have offered a change from the usual dabbling ducks and **American Bittern. Redtailed Hawk, American Kestrel and Barred Owl** are all quite common, and most of the commoner songbirds are well represented. The park gets quite crowded in summer, so an early morning visit is recommended. **Scarlet Tanagers** sometimes appear in late spring and summer, and **Bobolink** provides a splash of colour among the blackbird flocks in fall.

Most of the best birding is, however, south of town. Perhaps the best of all is on the Pinkney Point peninsula which lies on the other side of the Chebogue and Tusket Rivers from Chebogue Point. The salt marshes alongside Highway 334 are mainly covered with spartina which used to be cut for fodder and stacked in "stoddles". These now serve as perches for breeding farmland songbirds or hawks and owls which dispute the rights to meadow voles and shrews with raccoon, mink, red fox and river otter. A **Blue Grosbeak** in early May was an unusual spring sighting for the area which has a limited selection of breeding songbirds — the best of them being **Sharptailed Sparrow**. The arrival of the flashy **Willet** enlivens the scene, and the strangled gulps of courting **American Bittern** can provide an appropriate sound on a misty morning. **Wood Duck** may also nest in the area which has attracted a few **American Woodcock** whose youngsters may already be probing the ground for earthworms in mid May.

The marshes really come to life a little earlier during spring migration as **Great Blue Herons** flap in from the nearby colonies. Stray **Great, Snowy and Cattle Egrets** may also disturb the **Common Terns**, while parties of **Greater and Lesser Yellowlegs** pursue small fish on foot in company with airborne **Ringbilled and Bonaparte's Gulls** and swimming **Hooded Mergansers**. Other predators include **Northern Harrier** and a few elusive **Shorteared Owls**, both of which scatter the shorebirds from July on. The early flocks have included **200+ Shortbilled Dowitcher** before mid July, **Least and Semipalmated Sandpipers** and a handful of **Red Knot**. A mid August visit is more likely to reveal **Blackbellied Plover** flocks on the flats and **Lesser Golden Plover** in the marshes. The latest arrivals are **Whiterumped Sandpiper, Dunlin and Sanderling**, which stay well into November. **Peregrine and Merlin** take care of any birds venturing too far from cover at low tide. The inland woods provide habitat for many hardwood species. The upper sections of the Tusket River close to town are particularly attractive to **Whitebreasted Nuthatch, Veery and Rosebreasted Grosbeak**.

Swallows are very common along the river and may be joined by acrobatic **Common Nighthawks** in mid August. Large numbers of **Water Pipit** feed here in September and early October when the blackbird roosts can be quite large. They have usually left by the time the **Horned Lark, Snow Bunting and Lapland Longspur** flocks take over in early winter. November is a good month to see waterfowl. The last of the **Great Blue Herons** linger in the tidal pools, but soon **100+ Bufflehead, Common Goldeneye, Greater Scaup and Redbreasted Merganser** have arrived as winter sets in. The year is at an end when the **Roughlegged Hawk** assault on the small mammal population begins, with **Snowy Owl** as a distinct possibility, too.

The first large water area seen after turning off Highway 1 is that of the Melbourne Sanctuary. This provides a staging and wintering area for large flocks of **Canada Goose and Black Duck**, and smaller numbers of other species, including the rather local **American Wigeon and Bufflehead. Mallard, Greenwinged and Bluewinged Teals, and Northern Pintail** are all common on migration, and **Snow Goose, Gadwall, Eurasian Wigeon, Common Teal and Ruddy Duck** can also be looked for with some hope of success. Offshore parties of **Rednecked Grebe** appear in late November and February. The shallow inlet is favoured by **Ringbilled and Blackheaded Gulls** in fall and winter, and the spring flocks attracted a **Gullbilled Tern**. There have also been a few **Yellowcrowned Night Heron** sightings at Melbourne, which hosts up to **850 Shortbilled Dowitcher and 60 Willet** in late summer. The best songbird reported here was an early May **Loggerhead Shrike**—a rarity at any season now.

Once the mouth of the rivers comes into view, you can look for a long gravel bar reaching back northwards on the right. This, and the saltmarshes to the left, is Cook's Beach—one of the largest shorebird roosts in the region. One visitor has remarked on the spectacle of "great clouds of birds, mostly "peeps", flashing silver as they turned and banked, merging and separating" in a thrilling excitable mass as a **Northern Harrier** or small falcon appeared. As many as **5700 Semipalmated Sandpiper** rest here, along with up to **2600 Semipalmated Plover, 1100 Shortbilled Dowitcher, 170 Blackbellied Plover and 100 Least Sandpiper**. Most other species are also well-represented, including **Piping Plover, Ruddy Turnstone, Whimbrel, Hudsonian Godwit, Willet, Red Knot, Lesser Yellowlegs, Whiterumped and Pectoral Sandpipers. Ruff, Buffbreasted and Stilt Sandpipers** are also possible in fall, but the most amazing shorebird record is of **24 Dunlin** in early April—almost certainly the remnants of a wintering flock. A few pairs of **Semipalmated Plover** nest—one of few regular provincial sites, although **Willet** is the typical breeding shorebird of the marshes.

The last section of the road leads to Pinkney Point. Most birders forego a trip to the point itself and prefer to concentrate on the marshes and offshore waters just north of the community—this area is referred to locally as Pinkney's Point. The open water has **Common and Redthroated Loons, Rednecked and Horned Grebes** in early spring, and **Common Eider and Oldsquaw** most of the winter. The marshes are another feeding and roosting spot for shorebirds, especially if the flocks at Cook's Beach have been disturbed. Two **Stilt Sandpipers** recently appeared among the **100+ Shortbilled Dowitcher** congregation in mid July. **Peregrine and Merlin** often inspect the flocks in late summer and fall, when **Northern Harrier** is a regular visitor. Songbirds are scarce in summer—**Song and Savannah Sparrows** nest on the marsh edges while **Bank Swallows** return with insect food to their nesting colonies on the inshore islands. **Horned Lark and Snow Bunting** numbers build in late fall and a few of each usually winter.

The Salt Bay area offers a similar variety of species to those found in other parts of Yarmouth County. From Abrams River bridge through Eel Brook to Bear Road corner is less than a mile, but the woods on the northwest side and the bay off to the southeast provide good birding year round. Spring and fall offer the greatest selection, with **Ringbilled Gull** the most numerous resident. Mixed in with the flock are some bigger **Herring Gull** and a few **Blackheaded and Bonaparte's Gulls**. The swift waters of Adams River and Eel Brook are filled with small fish the gulls relish, as do the many **Doublecrested Cormorant** in the water. Large flocks of **Ringnecked Duck, Greater Scaup and Redbreasted Merganser** may be present in the area at times. **Willet** take up early summer residence, to be followed by **Belted Kingfisher**. Several **Great Blue Heron** fish these waters, along with an occasional **Snowy Egret** in spring and fall.

Just beyond Bear Road corner, a lane goes through deep woods to cross a marsh filled with **Redwinged Blackbird and Swamp Sparrow** songs, plus an infrequent **Rusty Blackbird**. The dyke at the end of the lane has created a large sandflat extending well into Salt Bay. This is a favourite spot for shorebirds in late summer — especially **Semipalmated and Blackbellied Plovers, Ruddy Turnstone, Greater and Lesser Yellowlegs, Least and Semipalmated Sandpipers**. A number of **Shortbilled Dowitcher, Red Knot** and sometimes a **Ruff** join them as they stir up the shallows for food. An **Osprey** is usually seen overhead, and a **Bald Eagle** may also drop over from the Tusket River. **Redtailed and Sharpshinned Hawks** stay year round, and **Barred and Saw-whet Owls** have both been noted. The high grasses of the old saltmarsh may shelter a **Greenbacked Heron** in summer.

The earliest spring arrivals, sometimes in February, are waterfowl. **Greater Scaup** drift in large rafts on Salt Bay, with **Canada Geese** flying by and a few **Black Duck** on the far shore. By early April the **Redbreasted Merganser** numbers reach their peak at the estuary, later moving over to Eel Lake where they are outnumbered by **Common Merganser**. A few young **Common Tern** may be found crouching in the grass by the road bridge. A big rock on the left side of the bridge driving from Tusket is used as a perch by **Ringbilled, Great Blackbacked, Herring and Blackheaded Gulls** in summer until the shorebirds arrive and take it over at high tide. Most of the birds are **Semipalmated Plover and Semipalmated Sandpiper** which stand toe to toe, shoulder to shoulder, and share the roost with **Greater Yellowlegs** and whatever else can be fitted on to such a limited space.

Eel Lake is best seen from the Highway 3 causeway. **Common Merganser** outnumber all other ducks, but **American Wigeon** appear with a few rarer species in spring, and **Hooded Merganser** are probably regular in early May. **Tree Swallows** are abundant at this time, to be followed by a wide array of songbirds including **Gray Catbird and Bobolink**. The roadsides used to have large numbers of **Chipping Sparrow** on fall migration, but the Department of Highways policy of removing wildflowers has put an end to that. When the summer birds leave, the winter birds move in to replace them. Local feeders attract **Hairy and Downy Woodpeckers, Redbreasted Nuthatch, Evening Grosbeak, American Goldfinch and Pine Siskin**, and there are sometimes good numbers of **Common Redpoll**. Phyllis Dobson's feeder in Eel Brook has a full selection, and her multiflora hedge shelters and sustains lingering **American Robin, Purple Finch, Whitethroated, Song and American Tree Sparrows**. She has even reported some **Ruffed Grouse** moving skillfully through the thorns that smaller birds have difficulty avoiding.

A slightly out-of-the-way destination might be the Tuskets which can be reached from Lower Wedgeport. **Leach's Storm-petrel, Common, Arctic and Roseate Terns, Great Blackbacked and Herring Gulls, and Black Guillemot** all nest on the islands which at one time formed the "Principality of Outer Baldonia" — a shortlived but hilarious nation! The owner carried his joke to the extreme and received the support of nations like West Germany who accused Canada of acting to suppress the aspirations of its residents for independence. The only residents apart from the owner were sheep! The islands are now administered by the Nova Scotia Bird Society. **Willet** regularly nest and hawks use the islands as staging stops as **44 Broadwinged Hawk** in late September clearly indicate.

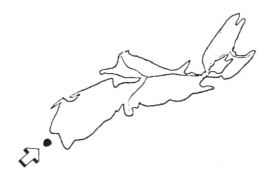

SEAL ISLAND

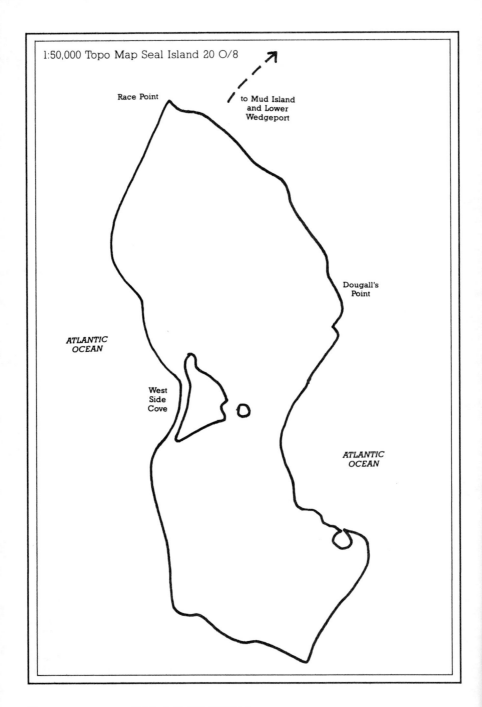

1:50,000 Topo Map Seal Island 20 O/8

Race Point

to Mud Island
and Lower
Wedgeport

Dougall's
Point

ATLANTIC
OCEAN

West
Side
Cove

ATLANTIC
OCEAN

There are three islands off Nova Scotia well known to birders. One is Sable Island which lies beyond the reach of most people; a second is Brier Island which receives visitors other than those interested in its birds; and the third is Seal Island which is of little interest to anyone except birders and the fishermen who take them to it. Several communities lie within easy reach of Seal Island; the closest are Lower Wood Harbour in Shelburne County and the Pubnicos, but the usual departure point is Lower Wedgeport at the end of Highway 334.

Seal Island is the first landfall for spring migrants and the last piece of land for birds on their way south, so it is not surprising that this treeless island would attract so many birds year round. It is also a magnet to birders, especially Bruce Mactavish who has spent several months on it in both spring and fall. Almost every bird species recorded in Nova Scotia has been seen here, and a few are Seal Island specialities. Large numbers of birds are a feature of September and early October when the accumulation of songbirds is unforgettable. A total of over 90 species is normal for both spring and fall.

Fall is generally the best time to visit Seal Island. The coastal configuration of southwestern Nova Scotia traps many migrants and encourages them to stay at feeders, but others, including the more exotic species, island hop this far to rest up for the longer crossing to Maine and beyond. Many birds head back north but the capricious winds and weather keep them here as choice morsels for the accompanying **Sharpshinned Hawks and Merlins**. The same situation occurs in spring when the birds are exhausted after a long sea crossing and have only the lobster pots to hide in before continuing their journey.

A winter visit is not recommended even if you can arrange for a boat, although there have been some notable "wrecks". The most famous was in 1968 — the year of **Black Skimmers and Laughing Gulls**, but this is probably one place that has some rare visitors every winter. Gulls and alcids certainly appear in good numbers in these waters and may include a few **Ivory and Sabine's Gulls**, and pelagics are also around until December when a few **Greater Shearwater** remain among the wintering **Northern Fulmars**. Both **Red and Rednecked Phalaropes** may stay into early winter, although the majority have dispersed long before then.

The first upturn in activity occurs in April when large numbers of diving ducks appear off the island. **Common Eider and Oldsquaw** are common at this time when strings of **Northern Gannets, Great and Doublecrested Cormorants** stream by. The first songbirds also appear in April with the earlier warblers and sparrows. An April storm is quite likely to deposit some unexpected southern strays snatched up from the Carolinas, but there is rarely anyone on Seal Island to greet them. Most spring visits have been made in May during the main migration. A mid-late May visit can uncover over a hundred species if a songbird movement is on.

Herons are particularly common visitors here. **Blackcrowned Night Herons** appear early and the early May **Great Blue Heron** migrants are soon followed by **Greenbacked Heron and Cattle Egret**. Shorebirds appear in small numbers, as does **Blackbilled Cuckoo** which is more often thought of as a fall migrant in Nova Scotia. Most of the flycatchers stop in here, including an occasional **Western Kingbird**, and **Roughwinged Swallows** are quite regular. The most unexpected hirundine visitors in late May have been **Cave Swallows** on at least two occasions. Other regular May migrants include **Brown Thrasher, House and Sedge Wrens, Wood Thrush, Bluegray Gnatcatcher** and a variety of stray warblers, finches and sparrows. **Bluewinged, Orangecrowned and Hooded Warblers** are quite frequently seen, and other notable visitors have included **Summer Tanager, Blue Grosbeak, Grasshopper, Field and Claycolored Sparrows**.

RB
1987

Blue-gray Gnatcatcher

Should the winds change and the mist and fog roll in, birds may be grounded for several days on Seal, and nearby Mud, Island. This is when the real rarities can be sought out. **Whip-poor-will and Great Crested Flycatcher** are not unexpected considering their breeding status in Nova Scotia but they are rarely seen on spring migration anywhere else. **Tricolored Heron** is rarely found anywhere in the province, but it has occurred here in spring, along with **Turkey Vulture, Upland and Stilt Sandpipers** — birds of the fall for the most part. The May parade of passerines has included **Wormeating, Prothonotary, Cerulean, Pine and Kentucky Warblers** — not a bad collection of vagrants on their own, but how about **Blackcowled Oriole, European Goldfinch, Greentailed Towhee and Cassin's Sparrow**? Numbers of all species are never as large as in fall, but **22 Field Sparrow** on one day in mid May suggests there are more birds in the Maritimes than summer records indicate. The last week of May brings large numbers of **Red Phalarope** and a few rarities such as **Laughing Gull and Longtailed Jaeger**.

Summer on Seal Island is much less frenetic, but the arrival of unusual birds should not be ruled out. Almost any heron or egret is likely, with a good chance of **Little Blue Heron** from birds raised in Massachusetts, and a summer **Purple Gallinule** shows that distance is no object. Geography is not a major factor either as a June **Glaucous Gull** clearly demonstrates. The most conspicuous summer residents are breeding gulls and the occasional nesting pairs of **Blackcrowned Night Heron**, but a few **Manx and Cory's Shearwaters** can be expected to wing by in June and July.

Without a doubt, fall is the most dynamic time of the year on Seal Island. Trips are best booked well in advance to avoid the mad rush to the dock with other birders. One of the main reasons for such enthusiasm to visit a lonely spot in the Atlantic is its ability to attract birds from all parts of North America within a few days of each other — it may be southern vagrants one day and then Arctic wanderers, a songbird or two from west of the Rockies, followed by an oceanic stray from far to the south. Because the birds are so tired and disoriented they rarely have the energy or inclination to escape the camera, and they have nowhere to hide if they do. The sheer volume of records for Seal Island from late August to early November points out the fact that any time is a good time to visit, although some species have a rather restricted schedule.

Early in the fall, during late August and early September, migration is dominated by stray landbirds and warblers caught up in the major movement along the Atlantic coast, and by shorebirds which are the main fall feature of the whole of Atlantic Canada. Seal Island has had more visits from **Roughwinged Swallow** than anywhere else, plus regular **Redheaded Woodpecker, Western Kingbird, Great Crested Flycatcher and Loggerhead Shrike**. There has even been a visit from a **Forktailed Flycatcher**, but it is usually the warblers that catch the eye. Almost every species found in eastern Canada has been seen here in late August and early September. **Prothonotary, Bluewinged, Cerulean, Prairie and Kentucky Warblers, and Yellowbreasted Chat** can be considered regular, and **Louisiana Waterthrush, Goldenwinged, Wormeating, Kentucky and Hooded Warblers** are all possible at this time. As if these birds didn't provide enough colour, **Bluegray Gnatcatcher, Yellowthroated Vireo and Orchard Oriole** add a few more.

Shorebirds seem to occupy every piece of real estate on the island. Flocks of **570 Lesser Golden Plover and 63 Hudsonian Godwit** at the end of August are maximum counts for the province. The birds aren't feeding, but they are alert to any change in the weather so they can continue their journey. With so many birds around, it is inevitable there will be a few rarities. **Upland, Buffbreasted and Western Sandpipers** are found most years, and an early September count of **12+ Baird's Sandpiper** indicates this species is not as rare as people think. The shorebirds peak at this time, and attention switches to other groups as the month continues.

By the end of August **Pomarine and Parasitic Jaegers** may appear offshore, and **Manx Shearwater** is almost certain to be found among the **thousands of Greater and Sooty Shearwaters** starting to return south at this time. **Yellowcrowned Night Heron** is quite likely to put in an appearance at the **Blackcrowned Night Heron** colony, but the most interesting visitors have been terns. **Roseate and Black Terns** are to be expected with the nesting **Common and Arctic Terns**, but at least two appearances by **Least Terns** are hard to explain. A few alcids trickle by in late August, when the first of several **Sora** appear. **Mourning Doves** are extremely common at this time and have included at least two **Whitewinged Dove** among their number.

The waters around the southwest tip of Nova Scotia can be teeming with pelagics in September. **2000 Greater Shearwater** is a normal count on the boat trip and most other species are represented. There has even been a **Brown Pelican** for variety and extra colour from the south. Groups of seaducks and alcids start to move by, although the peak migration does not start until October. **Cinnamon Teal and Common Moorhen** have put in rare appearances in early September, but it is the landbirds that draw the most attention. An odd **Turkey Vulture** may flap over, but two of the regular late September migrants are **Cooper's Hawk and Peregrine**. The latter was fortunately not around when a **Bandtailed Pigeon** found, or more accurately lost, its way here. There are always good numbers of **Yellowbilled and Blackbilled Cuckoos** late in the month when the **Western Kingbirds** might be joined by an occasional **Acadian Flycatcher** or even a **Say's Phoebe**.

Songbirds pass through in unbelievable numbers trying to beat the fall storms. **Bluegray Gnatcatcher** is a local speciality and the more usual **Warbling and Solitary Vireos** have been joined by a rare **White-eyed Vireo**. Warblers are very common, especially **Prairie and Orangecrowned Warblers**.

Other irregular visitors have included **Yellowthroated, Pine, Cerulean and Connecticut Warblers, Louisiana Waterthrush and Yellowbreasted Chat**. As many as **20 Northern Oriole** may be present at the same time which means a few **Orchard Oriole and Yellowheaded Blackbird** can be looked for, too. While **Summer Tanager** would be considered a notable find in fall, **Scarlet Tanager** is very common when the last of the warblers pass through. Sparrows begin to appear in good numbers at the end of the month with all the common species well represented. **Grasshopper, Lark and Claycolored Sparrows** are quite often seen into October, and there has even been a **Harris' Sparrow**.

When fall migration is reaching an end on the mainland, it is reaching its peak on Seal Island. The last **Doublecrested Cormorant** skeins can be seen heading by when the less orderly groups of **Great Blue Heron** appear. Pelagics undoubtedly feel at home in the stormy winds of October, as counts of **1500 Greater Shearwater, 400 Sooty Shearwater and 300 Northern Fulmar** clearly indicate. With so many birds to choose from, **7 Great Skua** on one October day is not as surprising as it might seem. There have also been **35 Redthroated Loon**, good numbers of eiders and scoters, and a few **Harlequin, Mallard and Wood Duck** for variety. **Blacklegged Kittiwake** flocks total over **2500** in late October when they may be joined by **Lesser Blackbacked and Ringbilled Gulls** and less hospitable **Pomarine Jaegers**. A **Sabine's Gull** was a welcome addition one mid October day.

The songbirds really have a hard time of it at this time. As many as **600 Sharpshinned Hawk, 150 Merlin** and assorted **Cooper's Hawk, Gyrfalcon, Peregrine and American Kestrel** all hang ready to make their move if they decide to head out over the water. Rails of all kinds are here, putting paid to the notion that they are poor flyers. **American Coot and Sora** are the most numerous, but **Virginia, King, Clapper and Yellow Rails** appear at times and **Common Moorhen** is becoming more regular. The later shorebirds rarely reach high counts, but a few **Upland, Solitary, Western and Baird's Sandpipers, Wilson's and Rednecked Phalaropes, Lesser Yellowlegs and Hudsonian Godwit** make a visit that much more pleasant. **Mourning Doves** are very common in October, when **Yellowbilled and Blackbilled Cuckoos** are joined by **American Nighthawk and Shorteared Owl**. The most common woodpecker is the **Northern Flicker**, although **Redheaded Woodpecker** is no longer considered unusual.

Western Kingbird is the most conspicuous flycatcher, but the commonest insectivores are the swallows which gather here much later than on the mainland. Eventually the flying insects disappear and so do the swallows, but a wealth of overwintering insects, midges and spiders among the lobster pots provide a good living for the many wrens passing through here. **Marsh and Sedge Wrens** are no longer a problem to find, and there are usually enough **Winter and House Wrens** to keep anyone happy. Seal Island has even turned up a few **Carolina Wren** and an early October **Rock Wren**. Another western stray later in the month was a **Townsend's Solitaire**. Perhaps the most surprising common species is the **Bluegray Gnatcatcher**—try to find them on the mainland and you're likely to strike out, but on Seal Island there have been as many as **30** passing through in October when most of the **Northern Mockingbird, Gray Catbird and Brown Thrasher** migrants leave.

The open windswept habitat appears perfect for the occasional **Northern Wheatear** that finds its way here in October, but other migrants are unlikely to relish the view. Vireos are found in higher numbers than on the mainland. **Philadelphia and Warbling Vireos** are quite common, and both **White-eyed and Yellowthroated Vireos** have also appeared. The warblers continue to stream through and October has been a banner month with **Swainson's and Blackthroated Gray Warblers** reported. At least one of every regular eastern species is likely to linger into October and numbers of some species are very high—**1000+ Yellowrumped and Palm Warblers** are a good example of this. Among the island's more regular migrants are **Prothonotary, Orange-crowned, Blackthroated Blue, Pine, Prairie, Connecticut and Hooded Warblers. Yellowbreasted Chat** is certainly increasing with **10** reported in just over a month one year.

Icterids are never common, but **Northern Oriole** numbers are steadily rising each fall, and there have been visits from **Eastern Meadowlark and Brewer's Blackbird**, as well as a fair number of **Dickcissel. Indigo Bunting** can now be considered quite common with early October counts of **20**, and **Northern Cardinal, Blue Grosbeak, Rufous-sided Towhee and House Finch** are also increasing. However, the top bird of October in this group has to be **Lark Bunting** which has appeared at least twice. The sparrows provide the bulk of the later migrants. As many as **2000 Whitethroated and 400 Whitecrowned Sparrows** may be counted on a single day in late October, and other species are also common. An amazing fall count of **90 Field Sparrow** one year underlines the ability of Seal Island to attract birds from all over the Maritimes. Several other species, including **Grasshopper and Claycolored Sparrows**, are also regular at the end of the month, and other less frequent visitors have included **Lark, Henslow's and Le Conte's Sparrows**. The flocks of **Horned Lark, Snow Bunting and Lapland Longspur** should not be ignored either as at least two **Chestnutcollared Longspur** have appeared in mid-late October.

Other places to visit from this site

On the way to Seal Island if you plan to leave from other than Lower Wedgeport, you will have an opportunity to turn off Highway 103 at intersections 32 and 31 to drive either side of Pubnico Harbour. This area is known for its rugged scenery and for its birds. From the turnoff at Argyle Highway 335 will lead you through Lower Argyle, Pubnico, Upper West, West, Middle West and Lower West Pubnico to the end of the road at St. Ann's Point. This is a good place to look for pelagics and for songbirds which are tempted to stay by the berries of the mountain ash trees found at the point. The other side of the harbour on Highway 3 takes you through East, North East, Centre East and Lower East Pubnico to Wood's Harbour.

This is one of the most productive birding areas in the province, partly because it is so close to Yarmouth and lies on the route of visiting birders heading towards other sites on the southern shore. Fishermen often report exhausted birds from the size of a **Yellowcrowned Night Heron** all the way down to **Rubythroated Hummingbird** landing on their decks. Spring starts as early as mid-late March, when **Canvasback, Mourning Dove and Threetoed Woodpecker** have been sighted and reaches its peak in late April-mid May. Up to **35 Rednecked Grebe** are a regular sight in mid April and some of the **150 Brant** that have stopped on Gull Island in early-mid May have stayed long enough to suggest they may eventually nest. **Blackcrowned Night and Greenbacked Herons, Cattle and Snowy Egrets, and Mute Swan** have all appeared on a regular basis, and other notable visitors have included late April **Gyrfalcon and Longeared Owl. Blackbilled and Yellowbilled Cuckoos, and Great Crested Flycatcher** have also turned up in spring, and there may even have been a **Chuck Will's Widow**. Songbirds are also common spring migrants, with **Eastern Bluebird, Philadelphia Vireo, Bluewinged Warbler, Northern Cardinal, House Finch, Rufous-sided Towhee and Vesper Sparrow** all regular visitors. This is also the best place in mainland Nova Scotia to see **Blue Grosbeak and Indigo Bunting** in April and early May.

Summer is a quiet time on the peninsula with the chug of fishing boats familiar enough to the nesting gulls and terns not to upset them too much. Twin Island, by Middle West Pubnico, has a small colony of **Roseate Tern**, and St. John's Island has **200 Common Eider nests**. There is also a **50 nest** colony of **Great Blue Heron** on Bond Island at Lower Argyle, and many of these birds feed along the peninsula in September.

Fall is the best time to visit in terms of numbers and variety. Waterbirds are not as common, but **Rednecked Grebe** again stage off this coast. Marshbirds are regular visitors to the coastal marshes with **Glossy Ibis, Blackcrowned Night and Little Blue Herons, Snowy Egret and Virginia Rail** all putting in an appearance. **Stilt and Western Sandpipers** have joined the commoner shorebird species. Birds of prey arrive in good numbers, including **Cooper's Hawk** in October, and the larger landbirds have included **Ringnecked Pheasant, Whip-poor-will and Redheaded Woodpecker**, but it is the songbirds that have provided the greatest number of rarities.

Western Kingbird, Northern Mockingbird, Gray Catbird, Brown Thrasher, Eastern Bluebird and Bluegray Gnatcatcher are all seen each year, and a count of **75 Eastern Kingbird** at Pubnico in mid September gives a good idea of the numbers involved. **Orangecrowned and Prairie Warblers** are among the more frequent of the rarer warblers, and other good migrants have included **Summer Tanager, Yellowheaded Blackbird, Dickcissel, Blackheaded and Blue Grosbeaks, Northern Cardinal, Rufous-sided Towhee, Indigo Bunting and Lark Sparrow**. Although winter can be pretty bleak here, the chance of seeing a stray **Clapper Rail or Laughing Gull**, or flushing an overwintering **Northern Cardinal or Pine Warbler**, should be enough to get any birder fortunate enough to be here out and about. **Snow Geese** have wintered around the harbour at Pubnico, but a small group of **Tree Swallow** found on the peninsula in mid December were less well-equipped to survive.

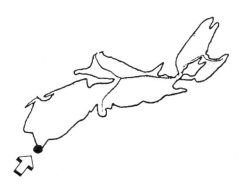

CAPE SABLE

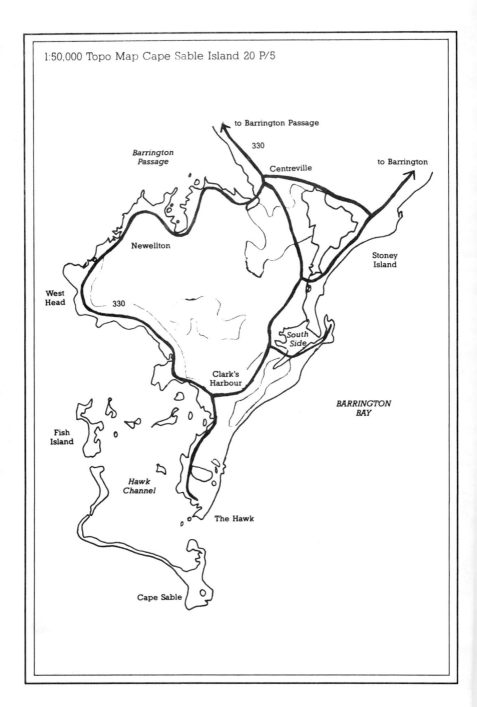

1:50,000 Topo Map Cape Sable Island 20 P/5

to Barrington Passage

330

*Barrington
Passage*

Centreville

to Barrington

Newellton

Stoney
Island

West
Head

330

*South
Side*

Clark's
Harbour

BARRINGTON
BAY

Fish
Island

*Hawk
Channel*

The Hawk

Cape Sable

Apart from the triumvirate of Sable, Seal and Brier Islands, this is the best place in Nova Scotia for rarities. One obvious reason is the location of the Cape and its island jutting further south than anywhere else in the province, but a more persuasive reason is the dedication of the lighthouse keeper's family who kept a weather eye out for birds as well as ships in trouble. Their first bird notes seemed so heady they were not believed, but the rarities kept coming and the Smiths have been shown to be correct in all their identifications. Over 300 species are on the area list, most of them on the small island where the lighthouse is located — a word of explanation here. Cape Sable is the island off The Hawk, which is the last point of land on Cape Sable Island — no longer an island since Highway 330 connects it to the mainland.

Highway 330 turns right off Highway 3 by Barrington Passage and passes through Centreville and Clark's Harbour where the mud flats attract marshbirds and shorebirds. **Blackcrowned Night Heron and Gullbilled Tern** have appeared in spring, and **Great and Snowy Egrets** have joined the gulls in fall when a **Laughing Gull** has also made a call. Shorebirds are quite common around The Hawk from late July when there are as many as **750 Shortbilled Dowitcher, 340 Semipalmated Sandpiper, 75 Sanderling, 45 Semipalmated Plover, 20 Willet** and a few **Piping and Lesser Golden Plovers, Greater Yellowlegs and Red Knot** to keep them company. The area has even persuaded as many as **75 Sanderling and 12 Ruddy Turnstone** to overwinter.

Perhaps the best birdwatching is on Cape Sable which becomes separated into two or more islands by storms. There were trees on the island, but most of Cape Sable is now dunes and marram grass and a few ponds to the east of the light where ducks and gulls rest. The Smiths have planted some trees and have some pasture, but their greatest contribution to the welfare of migrants have been the berry-bearing bushes and hardy native plants that provide food and cover. The island can be bleak and birdless one day, and covered with birds grounded by fog or storms the next. This is one place you can count on for birds after really bad weather.

Winter is, naturally, the least profitable time to visit the Cape. However, **100+ Horned Grebe** have been noted in late January, and you can always count on something unusual such as the **Eared Grebe** that swam in one January, a stray **Golden Eagle** in February, or a late-leaving **Killdeer or Blackbellied Plover**. There has even been a **Shortbilled Dowitcher** in midwinter, and **30 Sanderling** in April could also have been the remants of a wintering flock. Winter gulls are a distinct possibility, and there has been an **Ivory**

Gull here in addition to **Laughing and Sabine's Gulls**. An obviously lost **Peregrine** and a persistent **Shorteared Owl** did not find too much in the way of small songbirds, although **Water Pipits** usually overwinter and both **Yellowheaded Blackbird and Blue Grosbeak** have turned up in February and March. Midwinter **Western Kingbird and Tree Swallow** visitations would also have required a lot of searching for food. Perhaps the best of the late winter arrivals was a **Eurasian Jackdaw** — one of several in Atlantic Canada recently.

The Cape gets its share of early spring arrivals, although the spring is not really underway until the first **Brant** appear in April. The list of unusual visitors is not as long as in the fall, but there have been some real rarities like **Tricolored Heron, Blacknecked Stilt and Chestnutcollared Longspur. Greenbacked and Little Blue Herons** are quite regular from late April to mid May when **Snowy Egret and Glossy Ibis** can be looked for. **Sooty and Manx Shearwaters** often pass by inshore in May when as many as **1200 Red Phalaropes** have been counted. The seaduck passage is less conspicuous than other headlands, although **Harlequin** are regular in late April-early May. Gulls rarely stay long in spring when a **Gullbilled Tern** was a very rare visitor. Cape Sable is also one of the few places where shorebirds are common in spring. Up to **300 Blackbellied Plover** and smaller numbers of **Piping Plover, Ruddy Turnstone and Red Knot** return to the sandy beaches in May, when there have also been **Upland Sandpiper and Wilson's Phalarope**. Songbirds are sometimes grounded in storms but most make a very brief stop before heading north again. **Wood Thrush, Philadelphia Vireo, Rufous-sided Towhee and Indigo Bunting** are all regular visitors, and **House Wren, Yellowheaded Blackbird and Blue Grosbeak** have also paid visits.

Summer is also a busy time on the Cape as the inner beach has a **Common and Arctic Tern** colony which often attracts **Roseate Tern**. There are also several pairs of **Piping Plover** raising their young before late summer storms wash away part of the beach. **Willet** scream a warning on their way to nests on the Cape Sable Island marshes, but **Spotted Sandpiper** is the only other nesting shorebird. **Savannah and Sharptailed Sparrows** divvy up the dune and marsh grasses, and there is also a **200 pair Bank Swallow** colony which guarantees a few loyal pairs of **Cliff Swallow** and an occasional **Roughwinged Swallow** in early summer. Summer may also bring in an added bonus in terms of a **Little Blue or Blackcrowned Night Heron, Snowy Egret, White Ibis, Baird's Sandpiper or Rednecked Phalarope**.

Roseate Tern

The Cape is a revelation from early July to late October when the beaches are alive with frantically-feeding shorebirds. The high counts are indicative of the food available along the beaches. Counts of **1900 Semipalmated Plover, 520 Blackbellied Plover, 240 Ruddy Turnstone, 140 Willet, 100 Greater Yellowlegs, 100 Red Knot, 1500 Shortbilled Dowitcher, 200 Dunlin, 400 Least Sandpiper, 300 Whiterumped Sandpiper, 6700 Semipalmated Sandpiper and 1250 Sanderling** speak for themselves. **Whimbrel** and **Spotted Sandpiper** are also common in late summer, and there are usually small numbers of **Piping and Lesser Golden Plovers, Killdeer, Pectoral and Buffbreasted Sandpipers**. This is also one of the only places to lay claim to both **Snowy and Wilson's Plovers**, the latter on at least three occasions. **Solitary, Baird's and Western Sandpipers** are all fairly reliable in fall, while **Longbilled Dowitcher, Ruff, Upland and Curlew Sandpipers** are infrequent migrants, and **American Avocet** rather unusual.

Seabirds are another feature of the late summer and fall, and most pelagics are represented, including **Cory's Shearwater. Northern Gannet and Doublecrested Cormorant** remain until late October when waterfowl and marshbirds are very conspicuous. **Common Eider** is particularly common at this time and close inspection of the flocks may turn up a **King Eider** or two. Both **Blackcrowned and Yellowcrowned Night Herons** make irregular visits along with post-breeding **Little Blue Heron** and occasional **Great and Snowy Egrets**. The rails are also well-represented with **Sora, Clapper and Virginia Rails** most years, and **King Rail, Purple Gallinule and Common Moorhen** less frequently. While the few **Osprey** seen are usually summer residents, other birds of prey make a point of dropping by to check out the shorebirds and passerines. **Peregrine** is regular in mid fall, and **Gyrfalcon** has provided a bonus on several visits.

Passerines now have food and shelter to sustain them. Some species are more regular than others, but pretty well every bird on the mainland Nova Scotia list has found its way here at one time or another in fall. **Western Kingbird and Hooded Warbler** are local specialties, and so is **Yellowheaded Blackbird. Brown Thrasher** is another regular species and appears in large numbers considering its relative scarcity elsewhere — **60+** have been noted in less than two weeks in late September. An early November **Say's Phoebe** was perhaps the most interesting flycatcher seen here. Another of the Cape's regulars in October is the **House Wren**, and **Gray Catbird and Eastern Bluebird** are also frequent enough to be expected at this time.

Most warblers tend to arrive early in the last three weeks of August or late in the first three weeks of November. **Louisiana Waterthrush and Prairie Warbler** are regular among the early migrants, and **Yellowbreasted Chat, Cerulean and Kentucky Warblers** appear among the later birds. **Eastern Meadowlark and Dickcissel** are both present in mid-late fall when the sparrows take over. **Bachman's and Henslow's Sparrows, and Lark Bunting** rate the highest in rarity value, but late September-October **Blue Grosbeak, Claycolored, Lark and Field Sparrows** are more reliable. Cape Sable is also the best place to see parties of **Whitecrowned and Sharptailed Sparrows**.

Other places to visit from this site

Just off the community of Shag Harbour lies the subject of an award-winning book — Bon Portage Island. Evelyn Richardson brought it to national prominence when she wrote about her family life on the island, and it has remained in the news because of its birds. The province's first **Blackcrowned Night Heron** nest was discovered here and a January visit by **14 Fulvous Tree Ducks** has to be a highlight for anyone. The island comes into its own during migration when birds use it as a resting place. An early May **Turkey Vulture**, late May **Glossy Ibis**, as many as **5 Snowy Egret** together in late May, and **2 Field Sparrow** in mid month all deserve a mention. Other rare May visitors have included **Laughing Gull and Wormeating Warbler** — the latter extremely rare at any season on the mainland part of the province. This is also a good place to listen for nesting **Leach's Storm-petrels**

Bon Portage Island also holds a special attraction, for non-passerines in particular, in fall. Small parties of **Saw-whet Owl and Mourning Dove** have made use of the limited cover in mid-late October when early **Roughlegged Hawks** might have designs on them. There are lots of other choices for raptors earlier in the season. **Rubycrowned Kinglets** are abundant when the few **Cooper's Hawks** may fly by, and the later migrants usually have a few **Redeyed Vireo** and an occasional **Grasshopper Sparrow** among them. Other rare fall migrants here include **Bluegray Gnatcatcher, Wood Thrush, Yellowthroated and Philadelphia Vireos, Bluewinged and Prothonotary Warblers and Orchard Oriole**.

The next point east of Cape Sable Island can be reached by taking the turnoff from Highway 103 at Barrington just east of the Clyde River Bridge. The waters here attract large numbers of pelagics from late April, including **thousands of Northern Fulmar**, about a month after the main seaduck passage. **Virginia Rail and Rosebreasted Grosbeak** have been foolhardy enough to overwinter, and there have been a few spring **House Finches**. Nearby Brass Hill has had a **Western Kingbird** in June and **Roseate Terns** often fish in the harbour. The local farmlands also attract **Bobolink** in summer, and a few **Blackbilled Cuckoos** have found food enough to persuade them to stay a few weeks.

Barrington is a good place to look for unusual birds in fall. A **Least Tern** may have made it this far up Barrington Bay in late August and a group of **6 Gadwall** in late September was another good find. Other interesting fall migrants have included **Yellowcrowned Night Heron, Redbellied Woodpecker, Bluewinged Warbler and Blackheaded Grosbeak**, and there has also been an early September **Connecticut Warbler** — a species rarely encountered in the province. Although the local beaches do not have the numbers of neighbouring sites, a total of **120 Red Knot** on one visit is outstanding.

A short distance south from Barrington is the new Sand Hills Provincial Park with a variety of habitats including saltmarshes, tidal flats, sandspits, barrier beach, cranberry marsh and sand dunes. There has been little information so far on this site, but a mid September shorebird survey revealed **175 Blackbellied Plover, 75 Red Knot, 80 Semipalmated Sandpiper and 90 Sanderling** as well as a few **Semipalmated Plover, Ruddy Turnstone, Greater Yellowlegs and Shortbilled Dowitcher**. A few more visits would likely add more shorebirds and some passerines.

There are two good birding locations at Baccaro. Less than a mile to the east there is a small parking area by a copse of trees on the left and a path to Baccaro East. You can walk north along its edge to Crow's Neck where **Bank Swallows** nest in a low cliff. Between the beach and the lagoon there are usually nesting **Spotted Sandpiper** in June-early July, but it is wise not to disturb the **30+ pairs of Arctic Tern** which get even more annoyed when a **Pomarine Jaeger** makes a summer visit. **Piping Plover** sometimes summer, but they are more typically fall migrants with **Whimbrel** and the more common species. **Osprey** often fish here.

A little further on, the road bypasses the Royal Canadian Air Force station and leads to Baccaro Light. There is a parking lot just to the north of the lighthouse. The best birding is just to the south at Baccaro Point. **100 Great Cormorant** winter in the area with a few

Purple Sandpiper, and parties of **Rednecked Grebe** gather from late March. **Greater Shearwater and Wilson's Storm-petrel** often pass close to the point, and other species are possible in fog and early fall storms. The commonest ducks are **Common Eider,** which summer in the area and are very common in fall when a number of **Common Loon** join them.

Round Bay on the next peninsula to the east is known for its herons and egrets in spring. **Great Egret, Greenbacked and Little Blue Herons** are regular, and there has even been a very rare **Reddish Egret.** Shorebirds are less conspicuous, but an early July **Ruff,** late July **Stilt Sandpiper** and September **Marbled Godwit** indicate that a careful scan might pay off. Among the few songbirds reported, an early July **Roughwinged Swallow** rates a mention. The Cape Negro peninsula has a similar selection of habitats and probably the same birds.

Roswell and Constance Gallacher have a summer cottage near Shelburne, and they have provided detailed information on the breeding birds of the Clyde and Ohio River valleys. The Clyde can be driven on both sides north of Port Clyde and is an excellent river for boreal species. **Northern Goshawk, Spruce Grouse, Blackbacked Woodpecker, Olivesided Flycatcher and Boreal Chickadee** are widespread, and there is a good chance of adding **Common Snipe, Great Horned Owl and Pileated Woodpecker.** A few **Eastern Phoebe** nest along the river — one of the few places they can be counted on, and a **Rufous-sided Towhee** has been heard singing in mid June. **Piedbilled Grebe and Saw-whet Owl** are the only noteworthy birds outside the summer months. Permission to cross farm fields or use local roads should be sought as fire is a constant danger here.

The Ohio and Roseway Rivers north of Shelburne deserve a visit in spring, summer and fall. **Northern Goshawk and Great Horned Owl** nest, the latter showing an unusual preference for fish. Other summering owls have included **Longeared and Saw-whet Owls,** and there are often **Whip-poor-wills. Spruce Grouse** are widespread but hard to find, a trait shared with the nesting **Yellowbellied Sapsucker, Blackbacked and Pileated Woodpeckers. Olivesided Flycatcher** also nest, along with **Eastern Phoebe,** whose nests are often under river bridges where rare **Roughwinged Swallows** and a few loyal pairs of **Cliff Swallow** should be looked for in summer. Other summer visitors have included **Bobwhite, Eastern Bluebird, Warbling Vireo and Summer Tanager.** The fall is a good time to look for rarer migrants — **Eastern Bluebird and Blue Grosbeak** have dispelled the blues on some of the few visits made at this time.

The lakes and nearby Roseway River are good places to search for **Common Loon, Wood Duck, American Bittern, Common Snipe and Belted Kingfisher.** A canoe from one of the many local outfitters is the best way to see **Common Loon, Great Blue Heron, Greenwinged and Bluewinged Teal** at close range. Again, permission should be requested to cross farmland or use access roads.

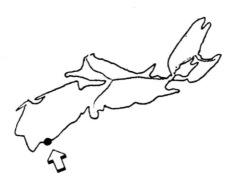

MATTHEWS LAKE

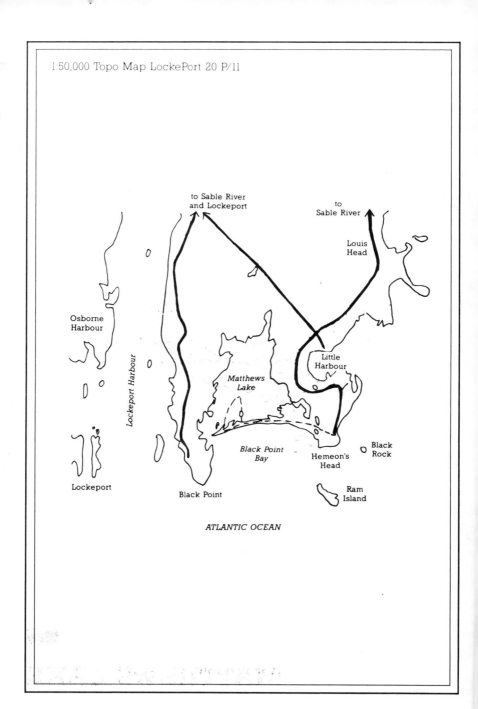

1:50,000 Topo Map LockePort 20 P/11

to Sable River
and Lockeport

to
Sable River

Louis
Head

Osborne
Harbour

Lockeport Harbour

Little
Harbour

Matthews
Lake

Black Point
Bay

Hemeon's
Head

Black
Rock

Lockeport

Black Point

Ram
Island

ATLANTIC OCEAN

Shelburne County is known for its fishing and farming and for its pleasant scenery, but it's also famous for its air of tranquility and its birds. The coast offers large numbers of shorebirds and good seabird watching. One of Nova Scotia's largest **Great Cormorant** colonies is found at Blue Gull Island, and most bird families are well represented. Some of the more notable rarities have included a summer **Northern Hawk-owl** and a **flock of Lark Buntings** in winter — somehow the seasons get mixed up here! The fall holds out most promise of rare birds, and nowhere is this more evident than at Matthews Lake which David Young now watches. Because I have visited this site only in early summer, I have relied on published reports and on a very thorough site guide he prepared for "Nova Scotia Birds".

Matthews Lake appears on older maps as Little Harbour Lake, and consists of a large marsh, beach and tidal lagoon. It is reached by turning off Highway 103 at exit 23 and driving just over 2 miles to the Little Harbour turn on the left. Another 7 miles brings you to the Little Harbour Country Store where you drive straight across for about 2 miles to the parking lot at Hemeon's Head. The Youngs live by a small cove on the left about a mile before the end of the road, the second last house is theirs. Black Rock and Ram Island usually have **Great and Doublecrested Cormorants, Common Eiders** and a selection of gulls most of the year, and a chance of offshore shearwaters, **Northern Fulmar, Red and Rednecked Phalaropes** in late summer and early fall. **Blackheaded Gull** is regular in winter and early spring and may eventually stay to nest with the **Roseate Terns** on Ram Island. **Thousands of Common Eiders** gather during the summer moult, and a parade of **Northern Gannet** is a feature of late September and October visits. The best birding is, however, at Matthews Lake to the west.

Follow the trail west from the parking lot along the beach for just over a mile to the mud and sand flats. There is usually a pair of **Semipalmated Plover** in the area and **Greater Yellowlegs** have nests not too far away. The first small ponds are good for up to **15 Common Snipe** in fall, and they also attract **American Bittern, Sora** and other rails. A small pond to the right — Teal Pond — is well-named for **Greenwinged and Bluewinged Teal** (with **50** of the latter in early September), **Black Duck, Mallard, Gadwall and Northern Pintail**. A pair of **American Wigeon** also stopped by in mid October. The lake itself also has **hundreds of Canada Geese** during the late fall and winter as well as **Common Goldeneye, Common and Redbreasted Mergansers**. David Young advises that this is not a place to be in the duck hunting season! Good numbers of **Brant** appear in spring.

An early September visit by a **Magnificent Frigatebird** is perhaps the best bird the area has offered, but David may find more. The timing of a visit is important if shorebirds are your target. The greatest numbers of birds are found on the flats to the north of the beach at low tide, which occurs over two hours after the tide is out at Lockeport and Halifax. You can walk on the flats for more than two hours before you have to make a decision to "sink or swim". Waterproof boots are recommended although the water and mud is less than ankle deep. At high tide the birds leave the area but a few may be found at Black Point or near the end of the spit.

As many as 27 shorebird species have been recorded here—about as high as anywhere in the Maritimes, but the totals are somewhat lower than the best sites. Nevertheless, **500 Semipalmated Plover, 275 Blackbellied Plover, 115 Willet, 105 Red Knot, 200 Pectoral Sandpiper, 330 Shortbilled Dowitcher, 175 Dunlin, 300 Least Sandpiper, 800 Semipalmated Sandpiper and 150 Sanderling** is far from shabby, although it is rare to find a thousand birds except in August and early September. **Hudsonian Godwit** is quite common in August, when **Piping Plover, Whimbrel and Lesser Yellowlegs** are also prominent and **Upland, Stilt, Buffbreasted, Baird's and Western Sandpipers** all possible into the first half of September. **Wilson's Phalarope** is becoming quite regular and **Eurasian Whimbrel, Longbilled Dowitcher and Curlew Sandpiper** have all been noted in September. **Whiterumped Sandpiper** is among the later migrants which have included **Lesser Golden Plover and Purple Sandpiper** on the headlands. The most recent addition to the area's shorebirds was not even in fall—an **American Oystercatcher** (or was it from Europe?) called by in late April.

Shorebirds are not the only attraction. **Snowy and Great Egrets** have been seen in late summer and the fall usually produces good numbers of raptors and songbirds. **Peregrine, Merlin and Northern Harrier** are often found hunting here, and the road and shore between Sable River and Hemeon's Head may yield a few good birds. So far, the best of the bunch have been **Western Kingbird, Summer Tanager, Northern Cardinal and Blue Grosbeak**. I took the West Middle Sable road and saw **Osprey, American Kestrel, Willet and Baybreasted Warbler** in summer.

The headland by the parking lot is also worth more than a passing glance. Hemeon's Head is an excellent spot to look for seabirds. **1000 Northern Gannet and 1500 Common Eider** call by in early August, and these birds are also a regular sight in early October, when as many as **100 Common Loon** congregate inshore. **Snow Geese** have also turned up at this time, and a little later there is a good chance of finding **Harlequin** and maybe even a **Tundra Swan** which made a surprise visit one Christmas. Most pelagics are brought in by fog and storms, although **Roseate Terns** in late summer and as many as **8 Wilson's Phalarope** about five miles offshore (?!) in late July probably chose to visit. Interesting spring visitors have included **2 Northern Shoveler** in mid April, **3 Gadwall** in mid May and a **Glossy Ibis** throughout that period. The best of the fall shorebirds is an **Upland Sandpiper** in mid August.

Little Harbour to the east has had as many as **35 Northern Fulmar** and a few **Cory's Shearwater** offshore in late September. Other outstanding sightings have included an early March **Canvasback**, early September **Whitewinged Dove**, and early November **Western Kingbird**.

Other places to visit from this site

The Lockeport Peninsula to the west of Matthews Lake is worth checking for vagrants. The one mile-long sandy beach and picturesque islands attract many visitors in summer, so the best birding is in the morning. **Piedbilled Grebe, Great and Snowy Egrets** are regular in spring, and there have even been visits from **Yellowcrowned Night Heron and Least Bittern**. Shorebirds also find the area attractive in April when **Willet, Lesser Yellowlegs and Shortbilled Dowitcher** have been reported. The best late April visitor was a songbird and a colorful one at that — **Prothonotary Warbler**. Both **Piping Plover and Willet** nest, and several **Glossy Ibis** and a **Mute Swan** offered contrasting colours in summer. Fall is a good time to visit for shorebirds, which have included **6 Buffbreasted Sandpiper** at West Head in early September. **Great Egret and Gadwall** have also been recorded in fall.

The approach to Matthews Lake is by way of Sable River which is surrounded by farmland. This makes it a good place to look for **Turkey Vulture, Gray Partridge, Western Kingbird and Purple Martin** in late summer. Other possible colonizers are **Brown Thrasher and Eastern Bluebird** — both of which have been seen in midsummer. **Willets** make a big splash in spring with as many as **150** in early May, when **Great Egret** is a strong possibility. Fall migration can also be spectacular, as a September flock of **1000+ Cedar Waxwing** and as many as **200 Bluewinged Teal** lingering into early October indicate. **Wood Duck and Hooded Merganser** are likely to be seen in late fall when the area's rarest visitor, a **Blackheaded Grosbeak**, appeared.

A few miles to the east of Sable River, the bays at Port Hebert and Port Joli have been made into a waterfowl sanctuary. The Port Hebert section is in Shelburne County, and its sheltered beach of white sand bordered by pine and spruce is near an old Micmac Indian campsite. **Piping Plover** breeds on the beach where there may also be a few **Common Eider**. Other nesting species on the slopes of Green Island include **Great and Doublecrested Cormorants, and Black Guillemot**. Most of the area is covered with coniferous forests and bogs where **Common Snipe, Gray Jay and Winter Wren** are relatively common.

The Sanctuary is, however, best known for its migrant waterfowl which reach high numbers in both spring and fall. Up to **4000 Canada Geese** stage here in mid October and many winter, while **Black Duck** total over **400** in May and twice that number in fall. Other common fall ducks are **Northern Pintail and Bluewinged Teal**, both of which occur in larger numbers than anywhere else but the Border Region. Later on **Greater Scaup and Common Goldeneye** are dominant, but there is usually a small wintering group of **Harlequin. American Wigeon** are more irregular in fall and **Brant** cackle their presence in spring.

This is also a good place for shorebirds in fall. Among the commoner birds, **600 Semipalmated Plover, 75 Willet, 160 Shortbilled Dowitcher, 400 Least Sandpiper, 500 Semipalmated Sandpiper and 1000 Rednecked Phalarope** are good counts for any site, and the proximity to Matthews Lake suggests rarer species are a possibility. There have been strays at other times of year, too, including an early winter **Cattle Egret**, and spring **Greenbacked Heron and Mourning Dove**. During the fall extravaganza astute observers have added **Yellowthroated and White-eyed Vireos** — hard-to-find vagrants anywhere in the province, **Prairie Warbler and Yellowbreasted Chat**. More visits would likely turn up greater numbers and variety of songbirds, but most people want shorebirds.

Neighbouring Port Joli Bird Sanctuary is in Queen's County and tends to attract fewer waterfowl and shorebirds. It does, however, have nesting **Osprey** and there has been a **Turkey Vulture** in mid April—perhaps a reminder of the ordeal awaiting some early residents who chose drowning rather than the alternative of walking barefoot on red-hot coals! Late in the fall it is worth looking for **Snow Goose and Redhead** among the large **Canada Goose** flock, which may be disturbed by a passing **Gyrfalcon** from mid October to late November. The most interesting songbirds have been several late-departing **Field Sparrows** and a mid April **Eastern Phoebe**.

Just beyond Port Joli is Cadden Beach which is shown as St. Catherines River Beach on earlier maps, and in brochures put out by Environment Canada. The area between the communities of St. Catherines River and Southwest Port Mouton is now the Seaside Adjunct of Kejimkujik National Park. The small park is dominated by the two white sand beaches, which are backed by tidal flats, brackish lagoons and saltmarshes. Bogs and ponds are common inland and there are large barrens on the adjoining headlands. Most of the coastal cover is white and black spruce, and balsam fir, but a scrubby forest of oak, aspen, maple and some conifers is found inland. Motorized vehicles are not permitted inside the park area which is reached by following an old cart track from St. Catherines River for just over a mile, or an old gravel road from Southwest Port Mouton for 3 miles.

While land mammals and seals are seen in the park it is best known for its birds. Large numbers of seaducks occur offshore, while dabbling ducks use the lagoons. A rare mid April visitor one year was a **Golden Eagle** who probably found the beaches bare. Gulls, terns and shorebirds nest along the beaches, but the area is best visited from August to October when the shorebird migration is on. Good counts here are **240 Least Sandpiper, 75 Sanderling and 65 Semipalmated Sandpiper. Semipalmated Plover and Shortbilled Dowitcher** are also regular, and **Whimbrel, Lesser Yellowlegs and Purple Sandpiper** can also be looked for in fall.

Its most famous shorebirds appear mainly in summer. This is the headquarters of the **Piping Plover** population with as many as **30 pairs** in summer either side of Black Point. Care should be taken as the birds can tolerate only limited disturbance before the young are flying in July. Their success is measured by the **100+** that may be seen together here in the early fall. **Willet** also breed in the neighbouring saltmarshes and **30+** may be seen in late August.

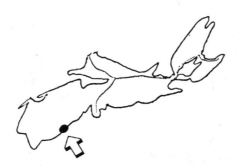

LUNENBURG COUNTY

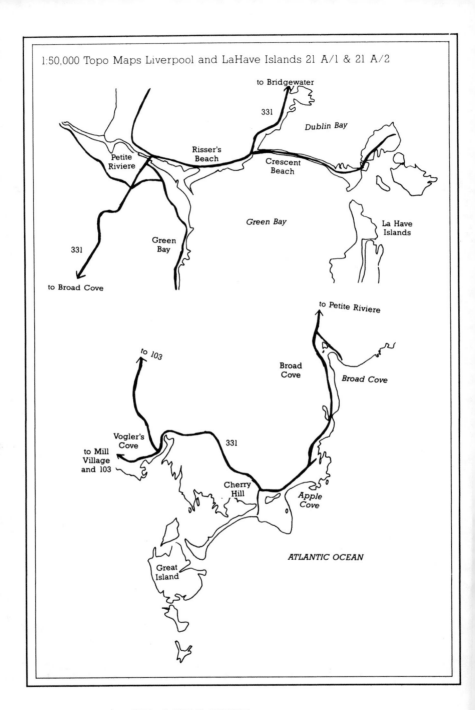

1:50,000 Topo Maps Liverpool and LaHave Islands 21 A/1 & 21 A/2

to Bridgewater

331

Dublin Bay

Risser's
Beach

Crescent
Beach

Petite
Riviere

Green Bay

La Have
Islands

331

Green
Bay

to Broad Cove

to Petite Riviere

to 103

Broad
Cove

Broad Cove

Vogler's
Cove

to Mill
Village
and 103

331

Cherry
Hill

Apple
Cove

ATLANTIC OCEAN

Great
Island

The shipbuilding prowess of Lunenburg County residents reached its peak with the building of *Bluenose* which outraced all other schooners until it retired undefeated. A replica *Bluenose II* now operates as the province's most visible tourist promotion, and other famous vessels of the rum-running and banking days are housed at the Fisheries Museum of the Atlantic in Lunenburg. Several other traditional reminders are also found in this region which is a popular tourist area.

Lunenburg County is also a very popular birding area, thanks to the coverage afforded by John, Shirley and Lise Cohrs, and Sylvia Fullerton, who spend as much time at their summer cottages in the area as in Halifax where they now live. There are several excellent beaches which attract a wide variety of ducks and shorebirds year round. This is the Maritime capital of "Willet World" in summer, and the Broad Cove Christmas Bird Count is the only real competition to the two Halifax counts for the highest provincial total each year.

The coastline can be divided into two sections. The first, which is approached by turning right off Highway 103 at exit 16 or 15 east of Mill Village, includes Cherry Hill and Broad Cove. Highway 331 takes you through Vogler's Cove to Cherry Hill. The beach is best reached by taking a right turn by the United Communities Fire Hall and driving to the pebble ridge. An alternative access is from Apple Cove by walking around the headland which is covered with gooseberry, huckleberry and blueberry bushes — definitely worth a visit in early fall. The best time to visit in fall, when the largest numbers and greatest variety of shorebirds is found, is low-mid tide when the birds are spread out on the mud flats, but if time is limited a better choice might be high tide when the birds are concentrated on the pebble ridges and limited marshland.

The first birds arrive in early July, and the spit and flats are covered with birds until mid October. Activity slackens but some of the best sightings have occured until late November. Numbers can be impressive with as many as **2500 Semipalmated Plover, 100 Blackbellied Plover, 70 Willet, 40 Red Knot, 105 Pectoral Sandpiper, 100 Shortbilled Dowitcher, 50 Dunlin, 80 Whiterumped Sandpiper, 275 Least Sandpiper, 530 Semipalmated Sandpiper, and 200 Sanderling** at times. **Whimbrel** are seen in good-size flocks feeding on the local crowberries, which also attract parties of **Lesser Golden Plover** later in the fall. **Piping Plover** prefer the sand beaches and are often seen among the **Sanderling** flocks, while the small groups of **Ruddy Turnstone** prefer the rocky sections of shoreline. **Pectoral Sandpiper** feed on the saltmarsh fringes where they are joined by **Buffbreasted, Stilt and Baird's Sandpipers**, all of which may appear in small numbers rather than as single birds.

Wilson's Phalarope and Hudsonian Godwit are regular at Cherry Hill, which has also had **2 Marbled Godwit** in mid September, a **Ruff** in early October and **Curlew Sandpiper** both in the striking summer plumage in early July and in more modest attire at the end of August. The main passage of immature **Whiterumped Sandpiper and Dunlin** is in late October and November when **Longbilled Dowitcher** has provided North American competition to a European invasion by **Eurasian Curlew, Eurasian Whimbrel, Ringed Plover and Ruff. Purple Sandpiper** would seem to be the most likely shorebirds, but **Dunlin** have attempted to overwinter, and **Blackbellied Plover, Ruddy Turnstone, Greater Yellowlegs and Sanderling** may also stay into December. **Piping Plover** often arrive back on the beaches as early as the end of March, and both **Red Knot and Pectoral Sandpiper** have dropped in for a brief visit in spring.

The coastline comes into its own in winter when the resident **Gray Jays** and flocks of wintering **Horned Lark, Lapland Longspur and Snow Bunting** can be flushed from the scrubby cover and boggy areas by the beach. The woods also keep a few **American Robin and Yellowrumped Warbler** into the winter months when they survive on the many berries along the shoreline. Some of the more notable landbird migrants have included **Peregrine, Blackbacked Woodpecker, Bluegray Gnatcatcher, Prairie Warbler and Yellowheaded Blackbird.**

The beach area and the small barachois pond by Apple Cove are well-utilized by gulls and terns which are often as numerous as the shorebirds. The late summer and early fall provide most of the interesting sightings—probably more as a result of the number of visits at this time than anything else. Apart from a few regular **Caspian Tern**, there have been a few **Gullbilled Tern** in summer with non-breeding **Roseate Tern** parties. **Bonaparte's Gull** turn up very early in fall and could be joined by an occasional **Sabine's Gull**. Storms in late fall and early winter have brought in **Laughing Gull, Sooty and Bridled Terns** from far to the south. A **Parasitic Jaeger** in March was in the right place at the wrong time.

Cherry Hill is also a good place to watch waterfowl. **Canada Goose, Common Goldeneye, Bufflehead and Greater Scaup** are the commonest over-wintering species, but groups of **Common Eider, Oldsquaw and Harlequin** can also be looked for in winter. **Gadwall** have also been seen in midwinter. The peak of **1000+ Black Scoter and 150 Rednecked Grebe** is reached in April when some of the hardier dabbling ducks return. In late September, the last of the **Bluewinged Teal** depart and the early winter concentration of **Common Loon, Rednecked Grebe, Great Cormorant and Northern Gannet** begins. The numbers begin to drop by mid November when the last of the **Whitewinged, Black and Surf Scoters** wing by. It was this time of year that produced a **Ruddy Duck** on the barachois pond.

The next community is Broad Cove, which generally lacks the variety of habitats that make Cherry Hill so attractive to birds. The most conspicuous winter birds are usually the odd **Bald Eagle** and the regular flock of **15-20 Harlequin**. There must be something special in the area, though, as both **Clapper Rail and Sedge Wren** have made very rare Christmas Count appearances. Spring is usually very quiet until the large flocks of **Common Eider and Black Scoter** pass by in May. This is also the time to look with some certainty of success for **Redthroated Loon, Snowy Egret and King Eider.**

Northern Gannet often pass by quite close, and the ponds and marshes around the community have good numbers of dabbling ducks throughout the summer and fall. A pair of **Hooded Merganser** have summered, and fall has produced a few **Peregrine**. Fall is the best time for songbirds, **Summer Tanager and Claycolored Sparrow** both having been found in September.

The next group of birding sites is reached by continuing along Highway 331 or by driving south on the same route from Bridgewater. The closest community to Broad Cove is Green Bay which is a very productive area for both waterfowl and songbirds. The bay attracts large numbers of **Common Loon and Black Scoter** in October, perhaps **200** and **100+**, and as many as **150 Common Loon** winter. These flocks are work checking as there are always **Redthroated Loon and King Eider** around, and a mid October sighting of an **Arctic Loon**. The wintering birds always include a few **Harlequin** which fly around like painted alcids looking for schools of fish or bob disconcertingly in the surf defying recognition.

Spring is very productive here with early April counts of **150 Common Loon, 500 Horned Grebe, 25+ Rednecked Grebe, 100 Oldsquaw, 40 Common Eider, 100 Surf and 300 Black Scoters** not unusual. By early May **Black Scoter** may top the **600** mark and there may also be **150 Whitewinged Scoter**, and the bay had enough of an attraction to lure **Horned Grebe and Surf Scoter** into summering. Birds of prey are also well-represented on migration with **Peregrine** most years and a party of **6 Redshouldered Hawk** late one September. Among other notable vagrants, **Yellowcrowned Night and Greenbacked Herons, King Eider, Ruddy Duck and Sooty Tern** stand out. Fall is also a good time to look for **Yellowbilled Cuckoo and Western Kingbird** which have appeared often enough to suggest they are regular. Songbirds can be quite abundant in fall as **500+ Blackcapped Chickadee** clearly indicate. Some of the more unusual sightings have included **Bluegray Gnatcatcher, Philadelphia Vireo, Orangecrowned and Prairie Warblers, and Indigo Bunting**. A few songbirds linger into winter, as late November records of **Water Pipit and Blackburnian Warbler** show, and the winter finches might include a **Hoary Redpoll** or two.

The next community is Petite Rivière, an attractive little fishing village where a good number of **Willet** make the most noise in summer. The breeding **Sharptailed Sparrows** also make a noise — I'd never call it a song, though! A **Yellowcrowned Night Heron** was a surprise visitor in early August and **Snowy Egret and Laughing Gull** have also appeared in summer, when the sheltered woods usually have a few **Pileated Wood-**

Shorebirds

pecker, Gray Jay, Pine Grosbeak and Whitewinged Crossbill as well as the more usual swallows, thrushes, warblers and sparrows.

The best time to visit is fall when the shorebird numbers peak and waterfowl are very common. **Peregrine** migrants usually have **Semipalmated, Blackbellied and Lesser Golden Plover, Ruddy Turnstone, Willet, Greater and Lesser Yellowlegs, Common Snipe** and a full range of sandpipers to choose from. The flocks of **Black Duck, Mallard, Northern Pintail, Greenwinged and Bluewinged Teal** have attracted **Eurasian Wigeon** on a number of occasions, but most of the wintering species arrive late. **Rednecked and Horned Grebe, Oldsquaw, Whitewinged, Black and Surf Scoters** and almost any alcid can be expected from November. A **Hooded Merganser** might also appear in February. Songbirds are also common in fall with **Field Sparrow** fairly regular migrants. Other notable finds include **Western Kingbird, Yellowbreasted Chat, Prothonotary and Orangecrowned Warblers and Summer Tanager**.

A quick early morning stop at Risser's Beach Provincial Park might be in order. **Eastern Meadowlark and Bobolink** often outperform the **Sharptailed Sparrows**, and nesting **Willet and Spotted Sandpiper** are joined by large numbers of **Sanderling and Whiterumped Sandpiper** on the long sandy beach. Gulls and terns are common, and there is sometimes a **Roseate Tern** in the feeding flocks. The salt marshes and white spruce are worth a check for migrant songbirds which have included **1500 American Goldfinch** in mid March! The most conspicuous birds after the shorebirds leave in fall are the diving ducks, with **Black Scoter** very common among the rafts offshore.

The last stop along this shoreline is often the most productive. Crescent Beach lies along a sand and mud flat bordered spit leading to the La Have Islands. It is a very popular spot with holidaymakers, but this doesn't deter the nesting **Piping Plover and Willet** which generally have their young on the move before July. Upwards of **50 Willet** are defended to mid August when the **Great Blue Heron** on the flats might be joined by **Yellowcrowned Night Heron, Great and Snowy Egrets**, all of which have appeared in summer. Both sides of the spit are worth checking — the ducks are found mainly offshore, while the shorebirds are inside the bar.

A count of **145 Willet** is quite a haul even for this shore, and **850 Semipalmated Plover, 110 Blackbellied Plover, 365 Shortbilled Dowitcher, 750 Semipalmated Sandpiper and 550 Sanderling** are not too shabby either. Above-average counts of **Piping Plover, Killdeer, Ruddy Turnstone, Whimbrel, Red Knot, Pectoral Sandpiper, Dunlin and Least Sandpiper** also occur during the peak migration periods. Vagrants are almost to be expected here, with regular visits from **Longbilled Dowitcher** and infrequent sightings of **Ruff, Buffbreasted and Stilt Sandpipers, and Wilson's Phalarope. Red and Rednecked Phalaropes** also pass by if the wind and water conditions are right. Most shorebirds, however, leave before the frosts, but **Dunlin** have over-wintered, and so have **Semipalmated Sandpiper**. Gulls and terns are also common in fall when **Ringbilled Gulls** may appear as early as late July and **Common Terns** may linger until early November.

A few marshbirds may join the **Great Blue Heron and American Bittern** feeding on and around the mud flats until October. A surprising **52 Mallard** have appeared in early October, and the flocks are now regular enough to suggest that the days of pure **Black Ducks** are threatened. There has also been a **Gadwall** among the commoner dabbling ducks. As many as **30 Redthroated Loon** have been counted in early November when the diving ducks raft in great numbers, with **Greater Scaup and Common Goldeneye** joined by a few **Redbreasted Merganser** and occasional **Barrow's Goldeneye and Lesser Scaup. Black Scoter and Greater Scaup** remain over the winter when most of the other waterfowl leave. A few **Dovekie** appear by November and there have been **Peregrine and Clapper Rail** in December and January.

Spring is heralded by a buildup in waterfowl numbers. **Common Loon** start to return offshore in March and up to **500 Common Goldeneye and 40 Rednecked Grebe** appear inshore with **100+ Horned Grebe** by mid April when the winter flock of **55+ Purple Sandpiper** is most conspicuous. Late in the month, as many as **400 Surf Scoter** may stay for a week or two with the last of the wintering and additional migrant **Black Scoter** rafts. Gulls become common again in mid May when a **Laughing Gull** arrived one year. The beachside trees sometimes trap migrants, and it is worth walking along the dunes and to flush warblers and sparrows sheltering in the grasses and berm along the shore. **Blackbilled Cuckoo, Eastern Meadowlark, Pine Warbler and Lark Sparrow** have been among the birds found this way.

Other places to visit from this area

The largest town in the area is Liverpool to the west which lies (naturally) at the mouth of the Mersey River. The brackish marshes and tidal pools along the coast attract **Doublecrested Cormorant and Great Blue Heron**, and both **Northern Harrier and Osprey** are quite common. There have been summer reports of **Snowy Egret and Turkey Vulture,** while the varied stands of hardwoods and softwoods support a high breeding population of both **Gray Jay and Veery** among the commoner species. Some of the birds arriving in spring stay to breed, including **Gray Catbird and Northern Cardinal**. Other birds bringing colour to a drab spring morning have been **Varied Thrush, Scarlet Tanager, Blue Grosbeak, House Finch**, and a number of April-May **Indigo Buntings**. Large numbers of **Common Goldeneye, Common and Redbreasted Mergansers** join the small contingent of wintering **Great Cormorant** near the rivermouth. A few **Rufous-sided Towhees** have been seen in late November and may winter, but the most exciting sighting for local residents was a flock of **120 Bohemian Waxwing** one winter. Nearby Mill Village has a similar selection of birds year round, and has added **Wood Thrush and Indigo Bunting** in summer. Bridgewater residents recently found **Hoary Redpoll** among the late February finches.

The east side of the La Have River is a farming, rather than a fishing area, although the community of Kingsburg has a fishplant where **Osprey** have overwintered. **Spruce Grouse** are quite common in the conifers, and **Cliff Swallow and Bobolink** are often seen around the fields. The best times to visit are during spring and fall migration. The western shore has **Snowy Egret and Indigo Bunting** most springs, and there has also been a rare mid May visit from a **Redbellied Woodpecker**. The most numerous migrants are, however, the **3500 Greater Scaup and 500 Common Goldeneye** that gather along the river. These rafts often attract **Surf Scoter and Lesser Scaup**. The fall is enlivened by flocks of migrant **Common Nighthawk** using the river as a southbound marker in August. There are also a few **Mallard and Hooded Merganser** by the river in fall. Further upstream near Baker Settlement I watched a July **Cattle Egret** living up to its name by picking flies and ticks off a herd of beef cattle.

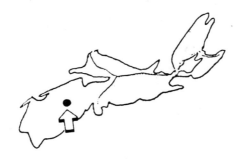

KEJIMKUJIK NATIONAL PARK

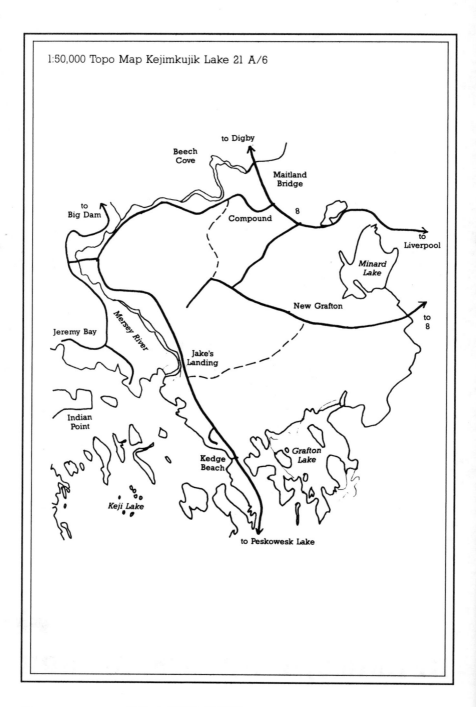

1:50,000 Topo Map Kejimkujik Lake 21 A/6

to Digby

Beech
Cove

Maitland
Bridge

to
Big Dam

Compound

8

to
Liverpool

Minard
Lake

Jeremy Bay

Mersey River

New Grafton

to
8

Jake's
Landing

Indian
Point

Grafton
Lake

Kedge
Beach

Keji Lake

to Peskowesk Lake

The only thing missing from Kejimkujik's habitats is a seacoast, but even that may be rectified by adding a section of coast along the Fundy shore. Freshwater plays a major role in the life of the park which has island-dotted lakes both large and small, a variety of rivers and streams, including the upper reaches of the Mersey River, and large areas of bogs and marshes. The many lakes resulted from glacial action which levelled the ancient hills into rounded shapes and allows some of the better hardwood stands in the province to flourish next to some of the oldest hemlock, red and white pines around. The range of habitats is best illustrated by the presence of ribbon snake, snapping and Blanding's turtles, and whitefish — relict populations in the waters, next to **Spruce Grouse, Saw-whet Owl and Blackbacked Woodpecker** — boreal representatives in the woods.

The large bogs and fens of the western part of the park are favoured by moose, while the more open mixed woods that cover two-thirds of the park are the domain of whitetailed deer. Although trails reach into most habitats, a canoe is the best way to enjoy the park's waterways. A number of **Common Loon** nest in the park and there are usually many other waterfowl in summer, but the park's main avifaunal features are its birds of prey and the juxtaposition of boreal and southern hardwood species. The closest location where this occurs is southern New Brunswick. The birdlife has been well-studied over the years and little has been added recently.

The most-visited and representative part of the park as far as its birds are concerned is the section alongside the Mersey River from the park entrance to Grafton Lake. You can walk along the river all the way to the roadbridge on Jeremy Bay Road, but it is better to study the upper section and then drive towards Jeremy Bay. In fall, a few **Bufflehead** stay on the river until freeze-up, and I have seen an **Osprey** here in mid February for a rare winter record. The first recommended area is to the right of the Administration Building. A trail leads over the river where **Hooded Merganser** certainly breed and **Wood Duck** are fairly regular in summer. A little further upstream towards Maitland Bridge a marshy area attracts **Greater Yellowlegs** from late summer, and **Solitary Sandpiper and Lesser Yellowlegs** at times in early fall. After crossing over on the floating bridge, it's best to take the trail to the right and look out for **Belted Kingfisher** and an occasional river otter. I have also heard a **Field Sparrow** singing here in summer, although other sparrows are more likely.

The trail then climbs away from the river into a small stand of white birch and then

Saw-whet Owl

into the only large stand of beech left in the park — which explains the Beech Grove trail name. Most trees bear evidence of the beech bark disease which has destroyed every other stand. The dead and dying trees offer food and nesting sites for one or more pairs of **Pileated Woodpecker**, and there are large numbers of **Least Flycatcher, Redeyed Vireo and Ovenbird** in the canopy. The north-facing slopes have more sugar maples and **Yellow-bellied Sapsucker** before the trail leads back down through a grove of tall shady eastern hemlock where **Blackthroated Green Warbler** wheeze a welcome. The first half of the trail often has whitetailed deer while the cooler slopes shelter porcupine and bats in the trees, and snakes and salamanders among the rocks.

Just beyond the Administration Building on the other side of the road is a turnoff to the Compound. While this area is off-limits, it is possible to walk along the old road to the park's southern boundary at New Grafton. This partly-overgrown trail has a good selection of breeding birds and migrants. **Saw-whet Owl and American Woodcock** certainly nest here, and the songs of **Whip-poor-will and Common Nighthawk** can be compared in summer. Most warblers commonly found in the park nest here, but the greatest number, including the very local **Nashville and Tennessee Warblers**, are found in fall. There is also a better-than-average chance of adding **Brown Creeper, Redbreasted and Whitebreasted Nuthatches** close to the Compound, especially during fall-early winter movements.

There are some small ponds alongside the trail and just before the New Grafton road. These have yielded **Mallard, Bluewinged Teal and Wood Duck** in spring and fall, and nesting **Belted Kingfisher and Redwinged Blackbird** in summer. The farmland alongside the New Grafton road may add **Common Grackle and Bobolink**, and there have been enough summer sightings of **Mourning Dove, Eastern Bluebird, Eastern Meadowlark and Indigo Bunting** to suggest they also nest. **Redtailed Hawk and American Kestrel** are both common, and **Broadwinged Hawk and Sharpshinned Hawk** are seen enough to indicate nesting.

The forested area at the intersection of the main park highway and the Jeremy Bay road is more boreal in nature than other easily accessible parts of the park. This is one of the best places to look for **Spruce Grouse**, which often bring their young close to the road, **Cooper's Hawk and Blackbacked Woodpecker**. It is also an ideal spot in the evening or early morning to listen for owls from April to early June. As many as **5 Saw-whet Owls** may be calling in the tamarack and spruce swamps, and an occasional **Longeared Owl** in the tall spruce and fir will mumble a reply to the monotonous toots of its tiny neighbours. Further away, the hoots of a **Barred Owl** from the campground may be forgotten as a **Great Horned Owl** booms a welcome from the Big Dam road conifers. Songbirds are not a major attraction here, although **Pine Grosbeak and Red Crossbill** are sometimes seen along the Mersey River and **Solitary Vireo and**

Blackthroated Green Warbler both nest. The roadside has one of the highest populations of porcupine I have ever seen—I counted as many as 25 from the kiosk to the main road one evening. Whitetailed deer and bobcat are also regular visitors.

Jeremy Bay campground sometimes loses a few sites in the summer to nesting **Northern Goshawk and Barred Owl**—both of which can be hazardous to your health if you venture too close to the nest or young. Both **Gray and Blue Jays** lay claim to any food left for them, provided they are quick enough to get there before the ubiquitous red squirrels and eastern chipmunks. You can also expect nocturnal raids by raccoons and flying squirrels, but don't leave food out for the black bears—they won't let you ask for it back! The Indian Point parking lot is a good place to look for **Common Loon, Redbreasted Merganser and Osprey**, and the trail offers a good selection of singing thrushes, including **Veery**, on a summer's evening. The best trail is back along the shore to a marsh opposite Jake's Landing where **Blackcrowned Night Heron and American Bittern** may be seen. This trail goes through mixed woods and has **Common Nighthawk, Whip-poor-will, Baybreasted, Chestnutsided, Blackthroated Blue and Canada Warblers** as well as a good selection of the commoner species.

The next good birding trail is on the other side of the Mersey River where it empties into Kejimkujik (Keji) Lake. **American Bittern** are certain to be seen in summer, and other visitors may be **Doublecrested Cormorant, Blackcrowned Night Heron, Common and Black Terns**. A few ducks and shorebirds sometimes feed here, but the trail leading around the edge of the marsh is distinguished more by the variety of flycatchers and warblers. The Roger's Brook trail has good numbers of **Northern Parula and Blackthroated Blue Warbler**, and usually a few **Alder Flycatcher, Eastern Wood-pewee and Blackburnian Warbler**, too. This is one place where an **Eastern Phoebe or Great Crested Flycatcher** could be listened for.

The boreal woods on the opposite side of the road behind the trailer and Field Office are notable for the high number of **Boreal Chickadee, Hermit and Swainson's Thrushes**, and for their nesting **Blackbacked Woodpecker and Palm Warbler. Great Horned and Saw-whet Owls** are sometimes heard calling as late as July from the pine groves alongside the road opposite Jake's Landing. The fields also attract **Nashville Warbler and Bobolink** in summer. The wetter spots are the best places in the park to see frogs, including the rare mink frog, and snakes. Ribbon and smooth green snakes are regularly seen, although garter, redbellied and ringnecked snakes are the commonest species.

Grafton Lake at the end of the main road has several nesting pairs of **Osprey** which have become used to people, but any visit, especially by canoe, should be cleared with the interpretive staff. The nature trail offers the usual variety of mixed woods species, plus **Eastern Kingbird, Cliff and Tree Swallows, Whitebreasted Nuthatch and Redwinged Blackbird. Great Horned Owls** sometimes hang around the bridge—possibly looking for fish like birds in Yarmouth and Shelburne Counties. This is also an excellent area for flycatchers. **Least Flycatcher and Eastern Wood-pewee** prefer the tall birches, and an occasional **Great Crested Flycatcher** may fly over or sing out a greeting from a distance. **Olivesided and Alder Flycatchers** are quite common along the Grafton Lake shoreline, where an **Eastern Phoebe** may also be heard. **Scarlet Tanager** is another possibility flying over or in the shade trees.

Other places to visit from this site

The nearest larger community to the park is Caledonia which lies along Highway 8 from Liverpool. The area between here and Harmony is mainly hardwood and small ponds, and the nesting birds reflect this. **Wood Duck and Common Moorhen** summer and may well nest, and there have been several broods of **Ringnecked Duck and Hooded Merganser** with the dabbling ducks in late July. **Little Blue Heron and Cattle Egret** have also been seen in the latter part of the summer when the hazy days bring flocks of **Common Nighthawk**. A roost of **Chimney Swift** has been discovered in an old smokestack at Harmony, and **Wood Thrush** quite often nest in this area, but pride of place has to go to the **Goldencrowned Sparrow** which wintered at Thelma Bower's feeder at Turtle Lake. Other feeders have attracted **Gray and Blue Jays, Whitebreasted and Redbreasted Nuthatches**.

The country roads north of Maitland Bridge have good numbers of open country species such as **Bobolink and Indigo Bunting**, and other recent colonizers have been **Rosebreasted Grosbeak and Field Sparrow**. A few **Roughwinged Swallow and Eastern Phoebe** may appear in summer, although **Cliff Swallow and Eastern Kingbird** are more likely. **Common Nighthawks** are indeed common throughout this area, and there may also be a few **Whip-poor-will and American Woodcock. American Kestrel and Redtailed Hawk** are often seen overhead, while **Broadwinged, Cooper's and Sharpshinned Hawks** are irregular summer visitors.

A good area in the park is reached by taking the road to Big Dam which leaves the Jeremy Bay road where it turns sharp left to the campground. The mainly coniferous woods have bobcat and red fox as land predators and **Northern Goshawk, Merlin, Northern Harrier and Great Horned Owl** in the air. This is also a good place to look for **Spruce Grouse** and the more boreal songbirds, especially **Redbreasted Nuthatch and Pine Grosbeak**. Family parties of **Boreal Chickadee and Rubycrowned Kinglet** are very common in late summer with feeding groups of **Downy Woodpecker, Brown Creeper** and several warblers. The road leads to the Big Dam-Frozen Ocean canoe route, which offers the chance to see family groups of beaver and river otter, as well as **Common Loon and Common Merganser** at close range. The route also takes in the only remaining stand of mature eastern hemlock.

The last two areas that may be visited are accessible from the Peskowesk road. The first fork to the left leads to the hardwood stands around the firetower — the best habitat for a variety of woodpeckers, thrushes, warblers and finches. **Northern Flicker, Hairy and Downy Woodpeckers** nest every year, along with an occasional **Pileated Woodpecker and Yellowbellied Sapsucker**. There has even been a report of a **Redheaded Woodpecker** nest. Birch and maple are equally dominant and are the preferred sites of the small number of nesting **Great Crested Flycatcher and Scarlet Tanager**. All the park's nesting thrushes can be heard, including **Wood and Graycheeked Thrush**, neither of which is guaranteed. The dry heathy barrens off this road are the best place to find **American Woodcocks** which betray their presence with a distinctive late evening beeping call and a whistling songflight.

The Peskowesk road ends at Eel Weir where **Doublecrested Cormorant, Common Goldeneye and Common Merganser** are often present in summer and fall. This is also a good spot to look for **Tree, Barn and Cliff Swallows, and Belted Kingfisher**, as well as a good selection of songbirds, including **Philadelphia Vireo and American Redstart. Northern Waterthrush and Canada Warbler** are also commoner here than in other parts of the park. The bordering woods are more boreal and reflect the interior of the park. **Gray Jay and Common Raven** come to the campsite tables at Peskowesk Lake which is accessible only by canoe, and **Red and Whitewinged Crossbills** can often be heard overhead. One of the most powerful songs is that of the **Rubycrowned Kinglet** which is likely to receive competition from the **Winter Wren** now that its numbers are back to normal after a drop in the 1970s.

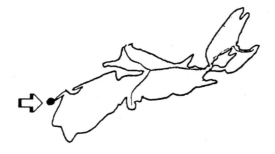

BRIER ISLAND

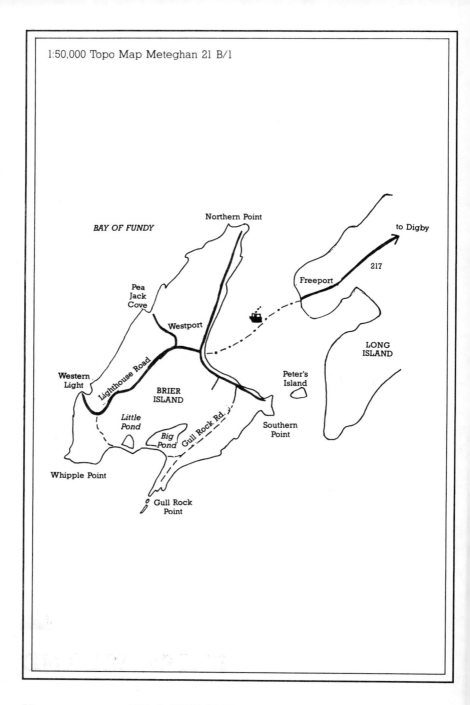

1:50,000 Topo Map Meteghan 21 B/1

BAY OF FUNDY

Northern Point

to Digby

217

Freeport

Pea
Jack
Cove

Westport

LONG
ISLAND

Western
Light

Lighthouse Road

BRIER
ISLAND

Peter's
Island

Little
Pond

Big
Pond

Gull Rock Rd.

Southern
Point

Whipple Point

Gull Rock
Point

The long peninsula pointing like an outstretched finger into the waters of the Bay of Fundy is one of the more unique habitats in the province. Highway 217 extends 40 miles through a succession of spruce and alder covered ridges, farmland, rocky coasts, sandy beaches and small ponds, and includes two short ferry crossings before Brier Island is finally reached. The ferry between East Ferry and Tiverton leaves on the half hour and returns on the hour, while that between Freeport and Westport leaves on the hour and returns just before the half hour. Both run on demand 24 hours a day year round with a nominal charge for vehicles, and are often crowded on summer weekends.

Although most of the island is public land there are few restrictions placed on access, and you can walk to most headlands with ease. The basalt cliffs on the island's south side are very similar to the Giant's Causeway in Ireland—it would take a giant to escape the surge of the onrushing Fundy tides! I haven't made the trip to Brier Island, but many Nova Scotia birders wouldn't feel their year complete without at least one visit. I have used the detailed description by Eric Mills to supplement published records in "Nova Scotia Birds" for a year-round guide to the different parts of the island, which is about 8 sq. miles in area.

The ferry docks at Westport which has enough cover to keep migrants and strays around for a few days. Even the ditches may hold sparrows and out-of-season warblers in early spring and late fall. Winter often brings a few surprising visitors to the feeders and any unfrozen ground by septic tank seepage. You can walk around the community to examine the weedy fields and check the feeders. A short walk to the northwest leads you to Pea Jack Cove after a careful check of the old, overgrown cemetery and a gravel pit. Seaducks, loons and grebes often shelter in the cove. You can then walk along the rough road to Northern Point.

If time is limited, turn right from the ferry wharf in Westport along the road to Northern Point. Some trails lead into several thickets and clearings where songbirds are quite common on migration. Northern Point itself is very active after a cold front passes in late summer or fall. Many migrants take off from here at dawn to fly north or northeast. The small spruce thickets and the lawn and bushes around the lighthouse often have grounded birds. Even more birds are found in the heavier growth to the south where the birdbanding trails provide the best access. Researchers from Acadia University in Wolfville have set up a full-scale operation here and there are usually a few good songbirds to report from August to late October. This area is most productive in September when the songbirds are in the open, but a few weeks of **Sharpshinned Hawk and Merlin** attacks tend to keep them more hidden. **Darkeyed Junco**, sparrows and winter finches are very common in October, and the next month brings more finches.

Seawatching is recommended from Northern Light, especially on the flood tide and in northerly winds. Large numbers of **Red and Rednecked Phalaropes, Sooty and Greater Shearwaters** gather to feed on plankton from August to September. **Manx Shearwater** are quite regular here, and **Pomarine and Parasitic Jaegers** may be joined by an occasional **Longtailed Jaeger** when terns are around. **Wilson's Storm-petrel and Atlantic Puffin** are seen, too.

To the left from Westport, Southern Point is less than a mile away with Peter's Island just offshore. The fishplant usually has gulls, while the marsh to the right and the shore on the left are good spots for herons, shorebirds and the rarer gulls. A lane to the right provides the best view of "The Big Meadow" in the centre of the island. Peter's Island has nesting **Common and Arctic Terns** from late May, and there are sometimes a few summering **Roseate Tern**. Eiders, alcids and loons swim by on the current in winter. Gull Rock Road runs almost 2 miles to Gull Cove, and its raspberry tangles are worth checking for cuckoos, flycatchers and songbirds. Gull Rock comes into its own in winter with a regular flock of **Purple Sandpiper** and small numbers of **Harlequin** offshore.

Lighthouse Road leads west out of Westport past the new cemetery which can be productive during migration. The powerlines and field edges should be checked for **American Kestrel and Eastern Bluebird**, especially in April and October, and for flycatchers, warblers and sparrows. The campground area just short of Western Light is good for passerines on migration, **Saw-whet Owl** for a brief period in early spring and in October, and soaring hawks, usually **Sharpshinned Hawk** but often a few **Broad-winged Hawk and Osprey**, in the main fall migration period. These woods can be filled with **Black-and-white, Cape May, Baybreasted and Blackburnian Warblers, and American Redstart** at the end of August, and the nasal twang of **Redbreasted Nuthatch** migrants is also evident. **Philadelphia Vireo and Prairie Warbler** may reward the persistent birder at this time.

Western Light is a good place to look for humpback and fin whales and for **Northern Gannet, Blacklegged Kittiwake, Red and Rednecked Phalaropes**, alcids and seaducks in windy fall weather. **Sooty and Greater Shearwaters** may be seen on the water feeding on plankton in fall, and all three jaegers are possible into early October. Lighthouse Cove to the north is a haven for dabbling ducks, **Rednecked Grebe, Common Eider and Brant**.

Some of the island's best birding is at Pond Cove and Big Pond, which can be reached from a trail south from Lighthouse Hill or west from Gull Rock Road. The cottages and raspberry thickets offer food and shelter to migrants, while Whipple Point is one of the best points to see ducks in winter. The Pond Cove Road trail leads first to the barachois beaches of Little Pond and then to Big Pond. Both are good for ducks and herons, but Big Pond is the place to see shorebirds when the water is low. A **Curlew Sandpiper** has appeared here as early as mid July, and **6 Stilt Sandpiper** arrived together in August. **Semipalmated Sandpiper** outnumber all other species, but all are represented, including **Red Knot**. Several **Stilt and Western Sandpipers** have been noted in September, when **Hudsonian Godwit, Longbilled Dowitcher and Wilson's Phalarope** have put in an appearance.

The rocks and piles of rotting seaweed both ends of Pond Cove are also favoured by shorebirds, especially **Buffbreasted and Baird's Sandpipers**, which can number **5** and **20** from the end of August into October. **Brant** often overwinter, and the inshore flock of summering **Common Eider** sometimes has a few surprises. Ducks, herons and shorebirds gather on the edge of The Big Meadow, but human disturbance is becoming a problem. This was probably the favoured location for an August **Upland Sandpiper**. The best gull seen along the beach in early fall was a **Mew Gull**.

Brier Island has something to offer the birder any time of year, although mid-September is the time to pick up most species and late May is not far behind if a songbird movement is on. Birders are now a recognized part of the community environment, but hunting and all-terrain vehicle use continue unabated, which has brought calls for part of the island to be declared an ecological reserve. The recent work on the province's Breeding Bird Atlas should fill the gap in knowledge of nesting birds.

Winter is the quietest time of year, but numbers are huge even then with **3000 + Blacklegged Kittiwake** and masses of wintering alcids. Northwest gales may bring these birds close to the points. The flocks of **Thickbilled Murre** almost defied analysis one year, and **Razorbill, Atlantic Puffin and Dovekie** are all regular. **100 Great Cormorant** have also been counted one Christmas, along with a few **Doublecrested Cormorant** and the odd **Northern Gannet**. Perhaps the most surprising winter visitors were single **Golden Eagle and Redshouldered Hawk**. The only wintering shorebird is also very common — **700 Purple Sandpiper** have been counted at the turn of the year. **500 + Snow Bunting** are bound to attract a few **Lapland Longspur** and perhaps a lingering sparrow, although most of both leave by December. **Hoary Redpolls** have also been noted in late December.

Spring is not as glamourous as fall in terms of numbers, but it can be exhilirating to walk to one of the points to watch **Northern Gannet and Common Eider** on the move in March. **Redthroated Loon** are very conspicuous in early April, when there may be as many as **7000 Northern Gannet** streaming by with small skeins of **Great Cormorant** and larger ones of **Brant**. Many **Brant** remain into May, by which time some **Snow Geese** may have joined the flock. **Harlequin** offshore and **Gadwall** inshore have also been noted in spring. By late March **Saw-whet Owl and American Woodcock** are in good voice, and southwesterly winds may deposit some southern herons and egrets. **Snowy and Cattle Egrets** quite often arrive in March, and there have been a few **Glossy Ibis, Greenbacked and Little Blue Herons. Golden Eagle** are also infrequent visitors in early spring.

May starts out as a quiet month on Brier Island. Shorebirds always drop by in early May when some of the wintering flock of **Purple Sandpiper** refuse to give up the rights to their beaches. Flocks of **50,000 + Rednecked Phalarope** are a feature of mid May, and **Lesser Golden Plover** are also regular visitors. Larids rarely reach large totals, but an occasional **Laughing Gull** and an even more surprising **Least Tern** provide a geographical contrast to the lingering **Iceland Gulls**. A few more herons and egrets may flap in, with **Yellowcrowned Night Heron** the most frequent at this time.

Songbirds may appear early in May, as counts of **40 Brown Creeper** and an assortment of rarer species like **Wood Thrush, Eastern Bluebird, Philadelphia and Whiteeyed Vireos, Goldenwinged and Wormeating Warblers, Orchard Oriole, Lark Bunting and Field Sparrow** indicate. However, the alders are slow to leaf out in the salt spray and warbler movements rarely occur before the third week of the month. A few song-birds may regularly arrive early, especially **House Finch, Blue Grosbeak and Indigo Bunting**, and exceptionally early **Orangecrowned and Hooded Warblers**, but the majority wait until mid-late May. These have included the first provincial **Eurasian Jackdaw, Blackbilled Magpie, Roughwinged Swallow, House and Sedge Wrens, Warbling Vireo, Yellowthroated Warbler and Lark Sparrow**.

Spring migration continues well into early June when **Acadian Flycatcher, Graycheeked Thrush, Yellowthroated Vireo, Yellowthroated Warbler, and Summer Tanager** may appear. By early July the island has its full complement of **Boreal Chickadee, Goldencrowned Kinglet, Blackpoll, Yellowrumped and Blackthroated Green Warblers** on nests, and the shrieks of **12 + Ringnecked Pheasant** in mid May must have been a lit-tle disturbing — enough perhaps to explain the **Turkey Vultures** that appear overhead at this time. **Great Skua** is a regular visitor in summer when **South Polar Skua** has been reported in the Bay of Fundy.

It must be admitted that fall is the season of most visits — by birders and birds! A good example of a Big Day was September 6, 1971 when Davis Finch led the charge to **123 species** with nothing rarer than a **Purple Martin and 2 Philadelphia Vireos**. Stay for a few days with the wind in the right direction and that fabled 200 mark is not too far away. The most noticeable early migrants are pelagics and shorebirds. As many as **5000 Red and 500 Rednecked Phalaropes** gather offshore by mid August to feed on plankton brought to the surface by the churning tides. They are joined by flocks of **5000 Greater, 4000 Sooty and 25 + Manx Shearwaters, and 300 + Wilson's Storm-petrel**, which naturally attracts **Parasitic and Pomarine Jaegers** — the latter arriving in mid July and hanging around until October. As many as **120 Atlantic Puffin** may arrive in mid August, along with a few **Common Murre**. Shorebirds pass through for three months, mostly around Pond Cove, and the numbers change from day to day.

There is sometimes a rush of passerines in mid-late August when the rarer species have included **Warbling Vireo, Bluewinged, Prothonotary and Yellowthroated Warblers**. More visits would probably raise the total to that at the end of the month which is the peak season for local birders — you can find as many as 20 afield at any one time along with a few vagrants from away and some amused bystanders! This is the time to beat the bushes (gently, please!) for the strays that are certain to appear. Every bird family has come up with a surprise. **Say's Phoebe, Northern Mockingbird, Brown Thrasher, Wood Thrush, Bluegray Gnatcatcher, Philadelphia and Yellowthroated Vireos** is a good haul for the month, but the warblers, icterids, finches and sparrows have added an odd many more. **Goldenwinged, Bluewinged, Orangecrowned, Yellowthroated, Blackthroated Gray, Prairie, Hooded and Kentucky Warblers, and Yellowbreasted Chat** is a collection anyone would be proud of. Add in **Yellowheaded and Brewer's Blackbirds, Western, Summer and Scarlet Tanagers, Dickcissel, Blue Grosbeak and Lark Sparrow** during the main migration in September and it's not surpris-ing birders spend their vacations here.

Even more impressive than the variety of songbirds are the sheer numbers of seabirds. The beginning of September has the peak numbers clearly visible from shore but best seen from a boat. As many as **20,000 Red Phalarope** gather here to feast on plankton, along with **10,000 Greater, 3000 Sooty and 150 Manx Shearwarers, and 100 Rednecked Phalarope**. There is always the chance of adding a **Pomarine or Parasitic Jaeger, Great Skua or Laughing Gull**, and there have been several **Caspian and Black Terns** and even an **Arctic Loon**. Ducks are also quite common with counts of **600 Common Eider** at the end of August. A few **Gadwall** may also appear at the same time as a stray **Green-backed Heron**.

Red Pharalope

Birds of prey are also common in September. **Sharpshinned Hawk, American Kestrel** and somewhat fewer **Merlin** deplete the southbound songbirds, and an occasional **Peregrine** may disturb the shorebirds. **Longeared and Saw-whet Owls** are probably more interested in nocturnal insects and mice, but the kettles of **Broadwinged and Redtailed Hawks** may have to pitch down with a rare **Redshouldered Hawk** or more regular **Turkey Vulture** if the wind or weather conditions aren't right. Several hundred birds can be seen drifting over to Brier Island at this time.

The excitement of migration can't last forever, and even on Brier Island there comes a time when the numbers start to fall, but the variety is still there in October-November. A few shearwaters and **Leach's Storm-petrel** continue to feed close to shore with **200+ Red Phalarope**, but the commonest birds are usually **Northern Gannet** which pass by here in their **hundreds** in October. **Great and Doublecrested Cormorants** arrive late with small rafts of **Surf and Black Scoter**, and a few **King Eider and Hooded Merganser** are regular. **Harlequin** appear in November when the last **Gadwall** and occasional **Common Moorhen** have already left, and an unexpected late fall visitor one year was a **Tundra Swan. Laughing Gull and Pomarine Jaeger** are also to be expected in October and early November.

The total number of birds of prey is lower in October, but there have been as many as **3000 Broadwinged Hawk** early in the month when weather is a major factor in migration. **Cooper's and Redshouldered Hawks** appear with the last migrant **Sharpshinned Hawk and American Kestrel** most years, and there may be a **Golden Eagle**. Later on the wintering **Redtailed and Roughlegged Hawks, Northern Harrier and Short-**

eared Owl contingents appear. Most passerines have left by early October, but **Black-billed Cuckoo, Barn Swallow, Northern Mockingbird, Brown Thrasher, Eastern Bluebird and House Wren** are all regularly seen at this time. The later warblers may include **Nashville, Blackthroated Blue, Cape May, and Baybreasted Warblers, and Yellowbreasted Chat**, and there are nearly always immature **Redeyed, Philadelphia and Solitary Vireos** arriving late. **Dickcissel, Northern Cardinal, Bobolink, Blue Grosbeak, Rufous-sided Towhee, Field and Sharptailed Sparrows** round out the rarities at this time.

Other places to visit from this site

The island on the other side of Grand Passage — Long Island, and the long peninsula leading to it are collectively known as Digby Neck. The powerlines and roadsides are often filled with migrants, especially in fall when birds may be forced to wait a few days before continuing south. As many as **300 Eastern Kingbird** have been counted this way in fall. Dartmouth Cove is popular with waterfowl and shorebirds, some **Brant and King Eider** remaining to winter. Birds of prey use the peninsula as a flight line, and there are often **Turkey Vulture and Broadwinged Hawk** in the air along Digby Neck in both spring and fall. On the east side of East Ferry, a marshy pond at Tiddville is popular with grebes, ducks and egrets in spring and late summer. **Ringnecked Duck** nest and **Great Egret and Greenbacked Heron** have been noted in summer, too.

Both ferry crossings offer chances to see **Blacklegged Kittiwake, Red and Rednecked Phalaropes** at close range in the passages. **Greater, Manx and Sooty Shearwaters** are often seen flying by, and **Great and Doublecrested Cormorants, Black Guillemot and Common Eider** are also common. Freeport has overwintering **Brant** in the harbour and up to **300** can be seen in the early April migration. **Western Sandpiper** and late August **Caspian and Royal Terns** have also been seen at Freeport.

I haven't birded Digby Neck, but I have been to the headland north of Digby known as Prim Point. Apart from the many **Greater and Sooty Shearwaters** offshore in summer and fall, there are always a few **Brant and King Eider** during winter and early spring. Numbers of **Brant** reach **400+** in mid April, and a few reappear in late October-December. **Ivory Gull** has also arrived here in mid April. A small group of late May **Roughwinged Swallow** may have been prospecting. Fall is probably the best season to look for songbirds, which have included **Redheaded Woodpecker, Eastern Bluebird and Orchard Oriole**, and rather more frequent **Western Kingbird**. Both **Turkey Vulture and Redshouldered Hawk** increasingly drift over the Bay of Fundy, and a more unusual visitor was a very young **Common Moorhen** — most likely from one of the Saint John, New Brunswick, marshes.

Normally Digby would not rate a mention as a good birding spot, but who can ignore a **Lesser Blackbacked Gull** that has appeared for at least **17 consecutive winters** from 1970. It arrives each year in October and leaves for parts unknown in April. The harbour is also an excellent place to look for **Horned Grebe, Greater Scaup and Oldsquaw**, all of which are common in fall and early winter, and a few **Rednecked Grebe, Bufflehead and King Eider** on a winter visit. The marshes bordering the tidal area are also favoured by herons. I saw only **Great Blue Heron** in late fall, but **Cattle Egret** is a regular visitor in spring.

The Bay of Fundy ferry is an excellent and cheap means of seeing pelagic birds, making three trips daily between Digby and Saint John. The crossing is best made between

July and September, but any season provides a good selection of birds. **10,000+ Greater Shearwater** and large numbers of **Sooty Shearwater** are possible from late August to mid October, and up to **1400 Northern Fulmar** have been counted in spring and summer with smaller numbers in winter. **Blacklegged Kittiwake and Thickbilled Murre** are by far the commonest wintering species.

The best mid July sighting so far must be **2 Blackbrowed Albatross. Longtailed Jaeger** are less frequent than **Pomarine and Parasitic Jaegers** but they may be seen in late summer and early fall, when both **South Polar and Great Skuas** are possible. As many as **50 Manx Shearwater** have been counted from the ferry, and **Little and Audubon's Shearwaters** have been reported on very rare occasions. **Laughing and Sabine's Gulls** are equally likely, and both **Caspian and Black Terns** regularly migrate by. Later in the fall flocks of **Common Eider and Whitewinged Scoter** usually have a few **Black and Surf Scoters, and King Eider** in attendance. Landbirds may use the ferry as a convenient means of transportation in foggy weather and storms.

The Bear River area a few miles southeast of Digby is known as the "Switzerland of Nova Scotia" and has many of its houses built on stilts. The long roadbridge is a good lookout for ducks. Winter is the best time to visit as flocks of **Common Goldeneye and Redbreasted Merganser** are joined by **300+ Bufflehead** and occasional **Barrow's Goldeneye**. The hills above the community are also a good place to scan for soaring birds of prey. **Bald and Golden Eagles** often winter with **Roughlegged and Redtailed Hawks, and Northern Harrier. Redshouldered Hawk and American Kestrel** are less regular.

Smith's Cove to the north off Highway 101 has **Black Duck** and up to **100 Bufflehead** from mid October. One of the commonest birds in early August is undoubtedly the **Willet** with totals of **100** not unexpected. The farming nature of the area explains the wintering **Ringnecked Pheasants** and the few fall **Eastern Bluebirds**. The better summer birds have included **Pileated Woodpecker, Eastern Phoebe, Gray Catbird and Evening Grosbeak**, and **Brown Thrashers** can be looked for in gardens and thickets in the fall.

Annapolis Royal goes back to the early days of settlement, as far back as 1605, and a visit to the historic community is recommended. Birds, however, are equally interesting year-round. The Annapolis Basin has as many as **150 Greater Scaup and 200 Bufflehead** in winter when a few **Barrow's Goldeneye** and even an occasional **Canvasback** appear. **Black Duck** may number in the hundreds later on, but mid October is the best time to see **Mallard, Bluewinged Teal and Lesser Scaup**. Fall and winter storms drive the waterfowl close to shore where **45 Rednecked Grebe** have been counted in late October when the first wintering ducks appear. There has even been a **Tundra Swan** in winter, but the most exciting visitor was not a waterbird at all, but a female **Greattailed Grackle** from the southwest United States. An early May **Blue Grosbeak** and late May **Eastern Meadowlark** pale in comparison.

The Annapolis Royal area offers an interesting variety of habitats for year-round birding. The main attraction in spring and fall is the marsh located within the town boundaries and managed by Ducks Unlimited. Hundreds of ducks, especially **Bufflehead, Black Duck, Greenwinged and Bluewinged Teal**, can be found here, along with a few rarer ducks, gulls and herons. **Snowy Egret and Yellowcrowned Night Heron** have both been noted. The marsh dykes can be reached by parking in the Historic Gardens parking lot on George Street. There is no fee from mid October to June and the gardens usually have some late **American Robin** and an occasional **Northern Mockingbird** to dispute ownership of the fruiting shrubs with large flocks of **Bohemian Waxwing**. The trail leads to a path through the grasses to the dykes. This can be a windy and muddy walk, so warm clothing and boots are recommended. The Annapolis causeway provides a good view of the basin which often has ducks and other waterfowl in winter. A **Snowy Owl** probably realized the tidal power plant would provide more mice and voles than before. Port Royal on the north shore of the Annapolis Basin offers views of the marsh and of the basin. The end of the road at Victoria Beach is an excellent spot to check seabirds in Digby Gut. **Oldsquaw** are the most numerous birds—gathering here in **thousands** at dusk. The roadside trees also shelter migrant songbirds.

To the north of Annapolis Royal, the Victoria-Hampton shoreline is a good place to look for ducks and gulls. One of the best locations is Parker's Cove which has rafts of **Whitewinged, Surf and Black Scoters** in early October, and good numbers of loons, grebes and seaducks in the winter. **Northern Gannet** have also been seen flying by in March—presumably taking the Bay of Fundy route and including a little overland migration near Sackville. **Redthroated Loon, King Eider and Harlequin** are also regular early winter and spring migrants. The farmlands have good numbers of **Ringnecked Pheasant and Cliff Swallow**, and there have been enough **Blackbilled Cuckoo, Orchard Oriole and Scarlet Tanager** records to make the copses a target for inspection.

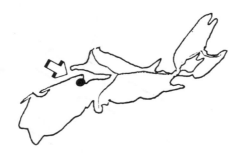

WOLFVILLE AREA

1:50,000 Topo Map Wolfville 21 H/1

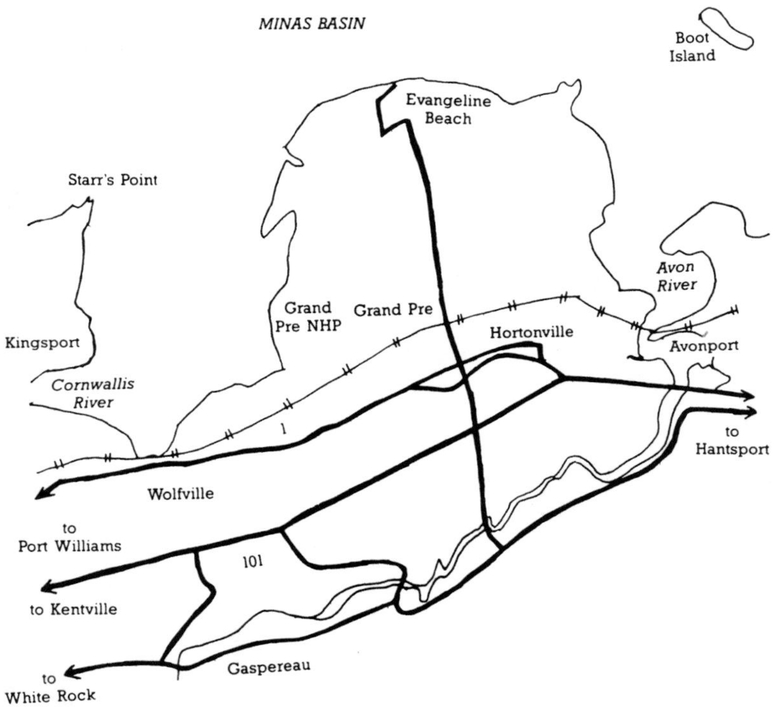

MINAS BASIN

Boot
Island

Evangeline
Beach

Starr's Point

Avon
River

Grand
Pre NHP   Grand Pre

Kingsport

Hortonville

Avonport

Cornwallis
River

1

to
Hantsport

Wolfville

to
Port Williams

101

to Kentville

to
White Rock

Gaspereau

Favourable climate and soil conditions have encouraged intensive agricultural production in the Annapolis Valley where the only remaining hardwood forests are on steeper hillsides and riversides. The only other forests are mainly coniferous which explains some of the boreal birds found in the region. The best-described area is around Wolfville where Peter Austin-Smith is a resident professor at Acadia University and Bernard Forsythe is an active birder on the Wolfville Ridge. The Minas Basin is a very important area for shorebirds, with about half of Atlantic Canada's migrants passing through in fall.

Wolfville's best-known birding resident, Robie Tufts, died recently, but his "Birds of Nova Scotia" is now in its third edition and a lasting memorial to someone who contributed so much to knowledge of the area's birds. One of the town's more unusual features has always been a colony of **200+ Chimney Swift** in the Acadia University chimney; a second roost of over **500** has recently been located in the Front Street Dairy chimney. At the other end of the year, large flocks of **Bohemian Waxwing** underline the town's university (I have always contended these birds are commonest in university towns where other bohemians tend to gather!). **Ringnecked Pheasant** also winter in small numbers, and the farming nature of the surrounding countryside is reflected in the **33 Gray Partridge** on the local Christmas count — many of them on Wolfville Ridge. **Northern Bobwhite, Barn Owl, Varied Thrush, Townsend's Solitaire and Sharptailed Sparrow** were even more unusual wintering birds.

As many as **80 Redtailed Hawk** and a few **Roughlegged Hawk and Northern Harrier** winter, and **Northern Goshawk, Gyrfalcon, Peregrine and Snowy Owl** are somewhat regular early winter and spring migrants. **House Finch** migrants may arrive in early April, about a month ahead of a rare **Purple Gallinule**. The spring has also turned up a large flock of **37 Glossy Ibis** one May — these birds were probably the forerunners of the nesting birds in New Brunswick. **Mallard** arrive in good numbers in spring and breed to the discomfort of later-arriving **Black Duck**. The town's shade trees are also a resting spot for songbirds, of which a late May **Scarlet Tanager** was one of the most colourful recently.

Wolfville Ridge north of town is the best place to look for birds of prey in summer. A **Redshouldered Hawk** has been seen in June, and **Barred, Shorteared and Longeared Owls** all nest. **Great Horned and Saw-whet Owls** may also appear on migration. This area has breeding **Alder and Least Flycatchers, Eastern Phoebe, Veery, Graycheeked**

Thrush, Chestnutsided Warbler and Evening Grosbeak. Wolfville itself has had unusual visitors in summer, including **Tropical Kingbird, Great Crested Flycatcher, House and Sedge Wrens**. Fall is probably just as exciting, although a mid October **Redheaded Woodpecker** is the only rarer bird I have seen noted.

Grand Pré is located to the northeast of Wolfville north of the railway line. The dykes were built by the early Acadians and the saltmarshes and estuaries have changed very little over the years. Breeding **Northern Harrier and Shorteared Owl** stay into winter when the regular **Shorteared Owl** roost may entertain as many as **12 Longeared Owl**. **Gyrfalcon and Peregrine** have also appeared in winter, and the resident **Bald Eagles** are given the luxury of carcasses and chicken parts to pick at all winter long. **Gray Partridge and Bobolink** also indicate the farmland nature of the area. Large feeding flocks of **Brant and Canada Goose** are a feature of spring, when there may be a few **Whitewinged Scoter** around, but the best time to visit is in fall.

Blackcrowned Night Heron, Cattle Egret and Sora turn up on the dykelands in late summer, and by late July there are flocks of shorebirds at high tide. **Northern Harrier and Merlin** are minor threats to the **Whimbrel and Lesser Yellowlegs** feeding in the fields, but they tend to make the **Mourning Doves and Blackbilled Cuckoos** even more difficult to find. Many of the **100 Semipalmated and 1500 Blackbellied Plovers** stay in the fields when other shorebirds leave for the mudflats, and in September they are joined by **600+ Lesser Golden Plover** and a few **Buffbreasted and Pectoral Sandpipers. Piping Plover, Upland Sandpiper and Ruff** may also be found feeding along the dyke edges.

Most of the other shorebirds only occur at high tide or in nocturnal roosts, but the numbers are very impressive with high counts of **20,000 Semipalmated Sandpiper, 1000 Shortbilled Dowitcher, 900 Sanderling, 270 Dunlin, 100 Willet, Red Knot and Whiterumped Sandpiper, and 25 Hudsonian Godwit**. Gulls are also quite common and a few herons may be seen until early October. **Yellowcrowned Night Heron and Franklin's Gull** in early-mid September are quite normal sightings. By late September, the numbers of shorebirds are much lower and ducks start to take over. **Common Eider and Whitewinged Scoter** are common in early November, and the geese feeding on the pastures should be checked for **Snow Goose**.

The low tide analogue of Grand Pré is Evangeline Beach at the end of a road to the north of the community of Grand Pré. **Great Blue Heron** nest in a colony at Boot Island with **Doublecrested Cormorant** and gulls. The mile-long beach is popular with summer visitors, but most people have left by the time the shorebirds take over in early fall. The gravel and sand beach attracts huge numbers of most species and is one of the main targets of local birders in August and September. Counts of **100 Hudsonian Godwit** in late July are unequalled anywhere else in the Maritimes. The commonest species in early August are **Semipalmated Sandpiper** with counts of **45,000, 1000 Semipalmated Plover, 200+ Red Knot, 100+ Blackbellied Plover, Dunlin, Shortbilled Dowitcher, Least and Whiterumped Sandpipers, and Sanderling**.

By late September the numbers are considerably reduced with **Blackbellied Plover, Sanderling and Dunlin** the commoner species remaining. A few **Shorteared and Longeared Owls** may join other birds of prey chasing the shorebirds, but the most conspicuous birds by October and early November are the rafts of **Common Eider and Whitewinged Scoter** offshore. As many as **20 Redthroated Loon** can be counted in mid November, but the most surprising winter total I have seen is of **29,000 Common Crow**.

The Avon River provides the boundary between King's and Hants Counties and is an excellent place to look for waterfowl and shorebirds in fall. The counts are rarely very high, but there is a good chance of totalling **5000+ Semipalmated Sandpiper, 500 Black-bellied and 300 Semipalmated Plovers** between Avonport and Cheverie. Other fairly common shorebirds are **Hudsonian Godwit, Willet, Ruddy Turnstone, Dunlin and Sanderling**. Herons and egrets are a possibility south of nearby Hantsport which is a farming community. Avonport has attracted a rare **Northern Wheatear** in late October and a wintering **House Finch**.

Other places to visit from this site
The farmland west and north of Wolfville is well worth visiting year round. Kentville is most productive in spring and fall, but summer visits have revealed a few **Upland Sandpiper** which might be expanding from the traditional New Brunswick sites. **Eastern Kingbird, Great Crested Flycatcher, Eastern Phoebe, Redbreasted and Whitebreasted Nuthatches, Rosebreasted Grosbeak and Fox Sparrow** all nest in the area, and numbers of **Bobolink** may be very high in late summer. The more unusual spring migrants have included **Snowy Egret, Glossy Ibis, Ruddy Duck and Yellowheaded Blackbird**, but the greatest numbers and variety are in fall. **Snow Geese** are regular, and **Northern Shoveler, Sora and Mew Gull** have turned a few heads.

Port Williams and Canard, especially the local poultry farm, are good places to look for ducks and shorebirds, including **Lesser Yellowlegs and Pectoral Sandpiper**. Most of the visits here have been made in fall, starting in mid August when young **Mallard and Bluewinged Teal** might be scattered by an occasional **Peregrine. Gadwall** are regular in September, and by mid October the local flock of **Doublecrested Cormorant** top the **300** mark, and for a month the seaduck rafts offshore may contain a few **Greater and Lesser Scaup**. Port Williams usually has a few early winter **Gray Partridge** feeding on the barren fields, but **Canada Geese** are the most conspicuous winter residents. Starr's Point has come up with a **Sora** nest, and the adults managed to successfully hatch 10 of the 12 eggs by mid June. A late May visit from **500 Brant** is not unusual here. **Northern Shoveler and Wilson's Phalarope** have also prospected the Port Williams area in May, and **Mallard** have already nested.

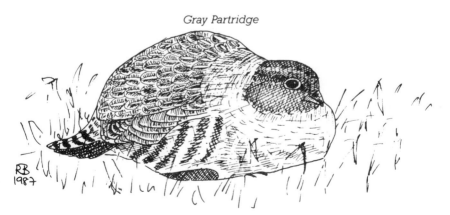

Gray Partridge

RB
1987

A short distance to the north off Highway 358, Canning and Kingsport offer a greater variety of ducks and large numbers of shorebirds in fall. A few **Virginia Rail** are around in late July when the shorebird flocks build, the highest counts I know being **26,000 Semipalmated Sandpiper, 840 Blackbellied Plover, 600 Shortbilled Dowitcher, 125 Semipalmated Plover and 42 Hudsonian Godwit. Gray Partridge** is a locally common year-round resident, and there are usually a few **Ringnecked Pheasant and Spruce Grouse**, and sometimes a **Bobwhite** or two, to keep them company. **Hooded Merganser** have been observed several times in the spring, and Canning is also the best place outside the Border Region to see a selection of dabbling ducks. **Gadwall, American Wigeon and Northern Shoveler** occur in small numbers from mid September to late October, when the **Doublecrested Cormorant** flock may exceed **500**, and there has also been a late **Little Blue Heron** at this time.

The last point of land to the north along Highway 358 ends at Cape Split. The view here is the finest in the province, allowing a look at six river valleys and parts of five counties. You can walk to the spit from Cape Blomidon through a number of forests before turning sharply down to a cove on the Scots Bay side. Depending on the state of the tide you can walk along the shore or take the clifftop path to the point. Don't get trapped at the foot of the cliffs — this is the Minas Basin with the highest tides in the world and they wait for no man!

The woods are filled with **Blackthroated Blue and Mourning Warblers** in spring, and the cutover area by the cove is a natural trap for migrants, especially warblers, **Redbreasted Nuthatch and Eastern Phoebe**. One of the earliest spring arrivals was a mid March **Yellowheaded Blackbird**, and a **Bluewinged Warbler** has been found in mid May during the start of the warbler migration. **Cooper's Hawk** often appears here after hawk movements across the Bay of Fundy and may nest as an additional songbird hazard to the usual breeding pairs of **Great Horned and Barred Owls. Evening Grosbeak** also nest in the woods — one of few sites in the province.

Two more places within easy reach of Wolfville require a short drive down Highway 12. One is most famous for its winter residents, the other has achieved fame for summer visitors. The first is Gaspereau Lake where Cyril Coldwell's eagle feeder has had upwards of **45 Bald Eagle**, regular **Redtailed Hawk, Northern Harrier and American Kestrel**, and occasional **Golden Eagle and Roughlegged Hawk**. A few strays have also been reported here — **Killdeer** in late March, **Orchard Oriole** in mid May and **Western Kingbird** in late September to name a few. The second place is Black River where Cyril Coldwell and Bernard Forsythe found an **Eastern Bluebird** nest in a rotting stump in the middle of a pond! This wooded area about a mile from the lake itself has been flooded, providing excellent habitat for nesting **American Bittern, Sora, Ringnecked Duck, Hooded Merganser, Common Snipe and Swamp Sparrow**. A **Virginia Rail** may also be present in summer and **Pileated Woodpeckers** quite often fly over. Flycatchers and warblers are very common in the wetter areas which can only be visited by canoe.

The final area that can be visited is southeast of Hantsport along the Meander Valley. C.R.K. Allen wrote an excellent account of this area in "Nova Scotia Birds" which I have used to supply a brief pen-picture. The river rises in wet conifer woods, but soon reaches rich farmland where it is bordered by ploughed fields and new hardwoods before the river widens into a floodplain with marine soils. Near its mouth, the Meander is tidal and has dykelands and hardwoods. The river valley is quietest in winter with boreal species in the upper woods hunted by **Northern Goshawk, Sharpshinned Hawk and Northern Shrike**. The upper hardwoods have resident **Ruffed Grouse and Pileated Woodpecker** and the berry crops are picked clean by **Cedar Waxwing and Pine Grosbeak**. Near the rivermouth, wintering **American Tree Sparrow** flocks have to watch for **Roughlegged Hawk and Shorteared Owl**, which may disturb a few ducks until freeze-up.

Spring is announced by the chirping of frogs at about the same time as the first **Canada Geese. American Woodcock** appear in the streamside thickets as early as mid March, soon to be followed by **American Robin and Song Sparrow**. The **Spotted Sandpiper** begins to trill a welcome in early May, and very soon after the main wave of warblers arrive. **Blackthroated Blue Warbler** come in the peak mid May rush to be followed by **Baybreasted and Mourning Warblers. Cape May Warbler and Northern Waterthrush** are commonest along the Little Meander, and the only **Sharptailed Sparrow** nests are in the saltmarshes of Ste. Croix. The best time for warblers is mid June when the songs are easy to pick out. **Nashville and Tennessee Warblers** prefer the upper reaches, and secondgrowth spruces attract **Magnolia, Baybreasted and Blackthroated Green Warblers**. Downstream hardwoods have **Ovenbird and Black-and-white Warbler**, and the middle reaches support the greatest variety of birds including **Yellowbellied Sapsucker and Gray Catbird**.

HALIFAX—DARTMOUTH

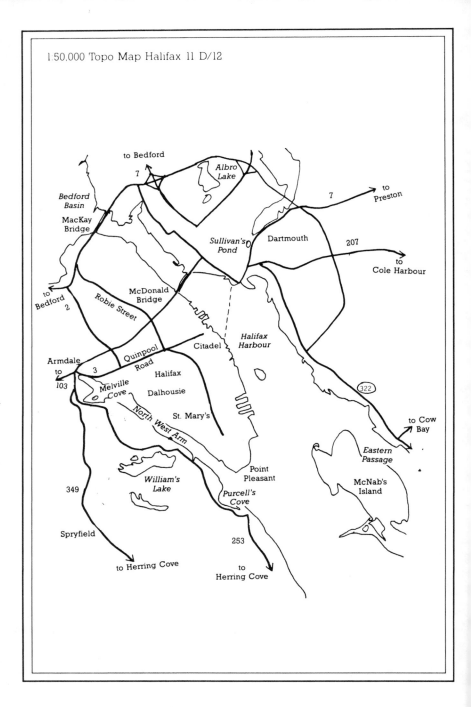

1:50,000 Topo Map Halifax 11 D/12

to Bedford

7

Albro Lake

Bedford Basin

to Preston

7

MacKay Bridge

Sullivan's Pond

Dartmouth

207

to Cole Harbour

to Bedford

2

McDonald Bridge

Robie Street

Halifax Harbour

Citadel

Armdale

to 103

3

Quinpool Road

Halifax

Dalhousie

322

Melville Cove

North West Arm

St. Mary's

to Cow Bay

Eastern Passage

349

William's Lake

Point Pleasant

McNab's Island

Spryfield

Purcell's Cove

253

to Herring Cove

to Herring Cove

The historic city of Halifax would probably never have reached such a high level of importance in English Canada if the French hadn't chosen to fortify Louisbourg in Cape Breton. Halifax has never been captured by any enemy, but it did suffer a tragic wartime disaster in World War I when a munitions ship exploded in Bedford Basin and left over 11,000 people dead or injured. The city's charm is retained in many of the original buildings and, more recently, in the reconstruction of the Historic Properties complex from where *Bluenose II* makes trips around the harbour.

Halifax is unique in having three universities within its city limits. I graduated from Dalhousie in 1975, and Mount St. Vincent's and St. Mary's are the other universities. While Halifax is the commercial and banking centre, Dartmouth, which lies across the harbour and is connected by two road bridges, is the residential choice of many birders. Both cities have excellent birding sites within their boundaries, and Spryfield is one of the better birding suburbs. I lived in Halifax for four years in the 1970s, but birding has come a long way since then, and I am amazed at the variety of birds now found within city limits. The two Halifax counts traditionally vie for the top spot on the provincial Christmas Bird Counts — many birds are found in town, although the Lawrencetown Circuit adds species to the Halifax East count and the Prospect area is a good source of rarities on the Halifax West count.

There are a number of avid birders living in Halifax, which partly explains the wealth of sightings year round. Reports at the monthly Nova Scotia Bird Society meetings held at the Nova Scotia Museum on Summer Street are always interesting regardless of the season. Feeders are now widespread, although the MacLaren and Cohrs feeders have provided many of the rarer sightings. For a while, the bird society bought seed wholesale for distribution, but numbers have apparently stabilized now and a local company handles all the orders. **Evening Grosbeak, Purple Finch, Pine Siskin and Brownheaded Cowbird** all appear in large numbers, and **Common Grackle and American Goldfinch** are perhaps more common than elsewhere, but the real attraction is the wealth of rare vagrants and lingering summer residents.

Redheaded and Redbellied Woodpeckers are appearing now and again to supplement the occasional **Blackbacked Woodpecker** straying in from outside the city, but a possible **Rufous Hummingbird** in early October did not stay long enough to be verified. Flocks of **Bohemian Waxwing** are regular in winter (why not with three universities!), and **Brown Thrasher and Northern Mockingbird** are regularly joined by

Bluegray Gnatcatcher, Rusty Blackbird and a dazzling collection of warblers, finches and sparrows. **Pine Warbler and Yellowbreasted Chat** can be considered regular, but **Orangecrowned, Magnolia and Hooded Warblers** have to be considered unusual, and a **Blackthroated Gray Warbler** downright astonishing. Among the better fringillids have been **Northern Cardinal, Blue Grosbeak, Hoary Redpoll, Dickcissel and Rufous-sided Towhee**. There are likely many other birds hidden away in some of the larger gardens close to Dalhousie and St. Mary's Universities. Dalhousie University's campus has had several fall **Pine Warblers**, plus **Great Crested Flycatcher, Eastern Phoebe and Northern Mockingbird**. A **Purple Gallinule** in early January was obviously lost.

Point Pleasant Park is one of the better places to study migration. Warblers are easily approached in May when they are more concerned about wandering dogs and hunting **Merlin**, which nest in the park. **House Wren, Warbling Vireo, Goldenwinged and Canada Warblers, Orchard Oriole and Field Sparrow** have all appeared at this time. Point Pleasant Park is also an ideal place to stroll around in winter when gull and waterfowl flocks include **Iceland and Blackheaded Gulls and Oldsquaw**. There have also been storm-blown **Leach's Storm-petrel and Dovekie** in early winter.

Northwest Arm which reaches from Ferguson's Cove to Armdale Rotary is a very pleasant drive or invigorating walk in the late fall and winter when waterfowl are present. The first cove from Armdale is the yachting harbour of Melville Cove, where parties of **Bufflehead, Oldsquaw and Common Goldeneye** are joined by **Iceland and Blackheaded Gulls** in winter. The arm produced a **Yellowcrowned Night Heron** from mid July to early August recently, and just beyond, the woods of William's Lake have regularly attracted **Whip-poor-will** in summer. The shoreline can yield **Common Merganser and Common Murre** from December to April. Flocks of wintering waterfowl at Purcell's Cove tend to be larger and more persistent, and there are often **Common Loon and Horned Grebe** close to shore.

Beyond the #16 bus route, the patient birder can expect to see good numbers of **Common Loon and Rednecked Grebe** along with some **Redthroated Loon and Horned Grebe** just past Ferguson's Cove. There are also alcids in the winter months with all species present at one time or another from November to March. The late fall offers a passage of seaducks and a few **Ringbilled and Blackheaded Gulls**. A side trip to York Redoubt brings **Greater Shearwater, Leach's Storm-petrel and Northern Gannet** if a movement is on. Rarer wanderers such as **Cory's Shearwater and Northern Fulmar** pass by in late summer.

The southern suburb of Spryfield still has a few woodlots left, but its rapid expansion may have eliminated most of my favourite birding spots. A rough walking trail led from behind the 500 block of Herring Cove Road to a shallow pond and conifers. The area is generally empty in winter except for the resident **Great Horned Owls** and a few sparrows, but it is very busy in spring and fall. I have noted 20 warblers on a day's stroll in May, and added **Purple Martin, Gray Catbird and Wood Thrush. Snowy Egret** is fairly regular in spring, sometimes as early as late March. **Saw-whet and Boreal Owls** have been recorded in April, but I doubt that my late February **Great Gray Owl** will ever be repeated.

The alders and mixed woods really come to life in the fall with large flocks of warblers in August and September. Parties of **Yellowrumped and Blackpoll Warblers** may reach

200 or more, and the birds should be carefully checked for other species. I have seen **Northern Parula, Goldenwinged, Orangecrowned, Pine, Mourning and Connecticut Warblers** here. **Philadelphia Vireo** is also regular in mid fall, when **Eastern Bluebird, Northern Oriole, Scarlet Tanager and Rosebreasted Grosbeak** may turn up. The pond also yields its share of rarer species with late summer and fall visits from **Great and Cattle Egrets, Common Moorhen and Sora**.

A large island in the middle of the approach to Halifax-Dartmouth is an excellent place to bird most of the year. A boat runs from Eastern Passage in Dartmouth and from Halifax, but further development is opposed by local birders who see the unspoiled beauty of McNab's Island being threatened. **Great Blue Heron** and the highest breeding concentration of **Osprey** nest on the island, and a marshy area usually has **Sharptailed Sparrow** nests. A recent visit in mid July produced **Doublecrested Cormorant, Black Duck, Greenwinged Teal**, 8 shorebirds, gulls, **Common and Arctic Terns**, and a wide variety of nesting songbirds including **Gray Catbird, Redeyed Vireo, Nashville Warbler, Northern Parula, Baybreasted Warbler, American Redstart and Rosebreasted Grosbeak**. The first of the wintering **Blackheaded Gulls** appear in September, when **Lesser Golden Plover and Solitary Sandpiper** are regular. **Whiterumped Sandpipers** are common in October when the first wintering **Purple Sandpiper** in winter plumage may cause temporary confusion. An August **Bluewinged Warbler** did not stay, but many warblers do, which explains **Black-and-white, Magnolia and Pine Warblers, and Yellowbreasted Chat** in mid-late December when sparrows are likely.

Halifax Harbour now receives a lot more attention since the Volvo plant became yet another regular wintering site for a **Lesser Blackbacked Gull. Bonaparte's and Blackheaded Gulls** flutter among the foraging **Glaucous and Iceland Gulls**, and there are occasionally **Laughing Gull** and late-leaving terns, too. Other interesting visitors to the waterfront have been **Tundra Swan, King Eider, Red and Rednecked Phalaropes, and Pomarine Jaeger. Ruddy Duck and Common Moorhen** have chosen Dartmouth Cove, and there have been some December visits from **Sandhill Crane, Hooded Merganser** and late-leaving **Sanderling**.

Lesser Blackbacked Gull

The sheltered extension of the harbour beyond the city limits is the best place to look for numbers of waterfowl and gulls in winter. Bedford Basin is a testament to man's ability to pollute anything at any time. The gulls don't mind and make the dumps and sewer outlets prime feeding areas. Large numbers of **Great Blackbacked, Herring and Iceland Gulls**, and parties of **Glaucous, Ringbilled, Bonaparte's and Blackheaded Gulls**, clean up the mess with help from an occasional **Lesser Blackbacked Gull**. Waterfowl are more finicky feeders, but **Common and Redthroated Loons, Rednecked and Horned Grebes, Oldsquaw, Common Goldeneye and Common Merganser** all find the murky waters full of food. **Ruddy Ducks** may appear briefly in fall and **Barrow's Goldeneye, Hooded Merganser and Thickbilled Murre** are regular in winter.

The adjoining shoreline has had its share of vagrants, especially the wooded grounds of Mount St. Vincent's University. You should, however, seek permission from the staff on duty if you want to prowl around the residence grounds with binoculars. The nuns may decide to have you arrested for more than vagrancy if you don't (and my middle name is Tom!). Among the many species legitimately reported are **Rufous Hummingbird, Blackbacked Woodpecker, Northern Oriole, Blue Grosbeak and Indigo Bunting**. There have also been very late-leaving **Rosebreasted Grosbeak and Vesper Sparrow**. The Rockingham area is another stronghold of the secretive but highly vocal **Whip-poor-will. Osprey** fish Bedford Basin in summer, and **Merlin and American Kestrel** may stay for the Christmas Bird Count.

What Dartmouth lacks in population it makes up for in birds. March is the best time to look for the first returning **American Kestrel**, and there may be a **Cooper's Hawk** in the air with the migrant **Sharpshinned Hawks**. There are not as many gardens or feeders as in Halifax but there have been enough excellent records to suggest that those in existence are well used. Some of the better winter visitors have been **Northern Mockingbird, Brown Thrasher, Marsh Wren, Orangecrowned and Pine Warblers, Yellowbreasted Chat, Yellowheaded Blackbird, Dickcissel and Rufous-sided Towhee**. The greatest activity is during the migration periods, especially in fall. Spring has brought **Great Crested Flycatcher, Warbling Vireo, Orchard Oriole and Indigo Bunting**, while **Northern Mockingbird** have stayed on to nest successfully.

Fall is the most productive time of year in urban Dartmouth. As many as **60 Blackheaded Gull** patrol the shorelines from mid September, when a **Yellowcrowned Night Heron** was an unusual addition, and the ferry crossing has yielded a few surprises like an early October **Leach's Storm-petrel** and early December **Dovekie. Western Kingbird, Yellowthroated and Philadelphia Vireos, Orangecrowned Warbler, Yellowbreasted Chat, Blue Grosbeak and Lark Sparrow** figure among the more unusual fall migrants.

The most productive spot in Dartmouth is Sullivan's Pond which proves that rare birds are no respecters of size or location. For some reason known only to the birds themselves, this little freshwater pond by a main road has attracted almost every duck known to occur in Atlantic Canada. The area was landscaped by the town to allow the introduction of domesticated waterfowl. The **Mute Swan, Canada Goose, Mallard and Black Duck** parties you see here are most likely domesticated, but the other birds almost certainly aren't.

Wild **Black Duck** — as many as **1000** — and **Mallard** do join the flock and there are usually some **Greenwinged Teal and Ringnecked Duck**. However, the real attraction to local birders are the rarities which seem to be growing each year. **Piedbilled Grebe, Gadwall, Wood Duck and American Coot** can almost be considered regular in fall and infrequent in spring. The two latter species may even overwinter if conditions are right. Other more unusual waterfowl have included **Snow Goose, Northern Shoveler, Common Teal, American Wigeon, Lesser Scaup, Ruddy Duck and Hooded Merganser**. This is also an excellent place to watch gulls, especially in winter. **Iceland, Ringbilled, Bonaparte's and Blackheaded Gulls** are present most winters, and **Lesser Blackbacked, Mew and Laughing Gulls** have recently appeared. There is little cover for songbirds, but **Lincoln's Sparrow** appears to be regular and a **Yellowheaded Blackbird** chose this site in late December.

Three other lakes worth a visit are on the outskirts of town. Russell Lake has **Greenwinged Teal** as an unusual urban nesting species, and **Northern Pintail, Ringnecked and Wood Ducks, Bufflehead and Hooded Merganser** on migration. **Willet** are the showiest of the shorebirds dropping by for brief visits in fall, when **Virginia Rail** is a possibility, but the only unusual wintering species have been **Piedbilled Grebe and Sora** — both doomed to failure, I suspect. There are more shrubs here, so regular **Eastern Phoebe** in spring, and **Bluewinged and Goldenwinged Warblers** in fall were well provided for. Morris and Albro Lakes quite often have waterfowl, especially **Hooded Merganser** in fall after any **Greenbacked and Little Blue Herons, and Cattle Egrets** have left. **Marsh Wren, Pine and Orangecrowned Warblers** are possible.

Other places to visit from this site

St. Margaret's Bay west of Halifax is a good area to watch for **Osprey** early in spring and in summer. The most conspicuous wintering waterfowl are **Horned Grebe and Oldsquaw**. The outer part of the bay by Peggy's Cove is too crowded to hope to see the few pairs of **Roseate Tern** that nest in the area, but Shad Bay and Prospect are worth a visit any time of year. This is a good coastline for pelagics, with **Northern Gannet** well into October and a few **Greater, Sooty, Manx**, and even **Cory's Shearwaters** in late summer. Shad Bay was the landing place for a very confused **Purple Gallinule** in late May, and at the other end of the year, **Common and Redthroated Loons, Rednecked and Horned Grebes, and Purple Sandpiper** are common in winter. **Roughwinged and Cliff Swallows, and Purple Martin** sometimes appear with the large flocks of **Tree, Bank and Barn Swallows** in summer, and another rare aerial insectivore was a **Western Kingbird** in late November.

Blake Maybank now lives at White's Lake, where he maintains a very active year-round feeding station. **Pine Siskin, Purple Finch, Evening Grosbeak and Darkeyed Junco** flocks are very large. One of the most interesting feeder occupants during my visit in June was a flying squirrel. Blake and I also turned up a good variety of warblers, thrushes and sparrows, plus a pair of nest-building **Gray Catbirds** and an out-of-place **White-breasted Nuthatch**.

A little closer to Halifax, Prospect Point is an excellent choice for a seawatch, especially in winter. **Northern Gannet, Razorbill, Thickbilled and Common Murres, and Dovekie** were all present when I undertook the Christmas Bird Count here, and I also had a group of wintering **Blackbellied Plover**. A winter storm may blow in a **Sabine's or Laughing Gull**, and I found an **Eastern Meadowlark** in the grasses by the point. Terrance Bay has **Great Cormorant** in winter, and an occasional **Hooded Merganser** in the shallows where **Iceland and Blackheaded Gulls** take their turns fishing. The most (fool)hardy bird I saw in midwinter was a **Ringnecked Pheasant** in the windswept heath by the lighthouse. The community feeders may turn up a late **Bobolink, Eastern Meadowlark or Dickcissel** among the flocks of **Common Grackle, Redwinged and Rusty Blackbirds, and Brownheaded Cowbird**, or a lingering **Northern Mockingbird or Northern Oriole**.

The closest peninsula to Spryfield is Cape Sambro and Chebucto Head where **hundreds** of stormblown **Black Skimmer and Laughing Gull** appeared in October 1968. More likely October visitors are **Caspian Tern and Doublecrested Cormorant**, which pass by in the main movement of **Northern Gannet** in their **thousands**. A few **Rednecked Phalarope** can also be looked for, but other shorebirds are rare along this rocky shoreline. Midwinter would be depressing if not for the active flocks of **Purple Sandpiper** and marauding **Glaucous and Iceland Gulls**. An **Ivory Gull** has appeared here more than once, and **Northern Gannet** sometimes fly by in winter. A female **King Eider** has also been noted in mid January. Songbirds are not a feature, although flocks of **Bohemian Waxwing** may be scattered by a **Northern Shrike**. The most interesting migrant reported is a **Cattle Egret** at Ketch Harbour in early May.

The small coves on the way to Spryfield are work checking for **Rednecked and Horned Grebes, Whitewinged Scoter, Black Guillemot and Dovekie** in winter. These birds sometimes come close to shore to shelter from the cold Atlantic winds. A mid April **Lesser Blackbacked Gull** may have had the same thought in mind. Songbirds also tend to rest up here in spring and fall. I have seen as many as 18 warblers in the coastal woods at Herring Cove, and the few feeders have persuaded **Yellowbreasted Chat, Chipping and Swamp Sparrows** to stay on past their time some winters.

The Sackville-Waverley area is still wooded enough to attract a good variety of birds year-round. Beaverbank has **Great Crested Flycatcher and Gray Catbird** in summer, and a **Bluegray Gnatcatcher** in June is evidence of better yet. My favourite location was Fall River on the shores of Fletcher Lake. This area of mainly secondgrowth produced several **Orangecrowned and Pine Warblers** on fall migration, and I suspect these birds are the ones that turn up in Halifax in time for Christmas. An early March **Yellowheaded Blackbird** and late May **Scarlet Tanager** are the best of the spring visitors, but **Yellowthroated Vireo and Wood Thrush** stay on to breed.

Susie Lake is not too far from here and is a very popular local spring migration spot. Good numbers of **Blackthroated Blue and Canada Warblers** appear in the main warbler wave. **Pileated Woodpecker, Whitebreasted Nuthatch and Yellowthroated Vireo** are local breeding specialities, while **Blackbacked Woodpecker and Purple Finch** indicate the presence of conifers. **Saw-whet Owl** may well be regular in summer, although the most conspicuous bird of prey is the **Osprey**. A stray **Little Blue Heron** appeared in late May and at least one pair of **Great Crested Flycatcher** have summered.

Mount Uniacke located north of Halifax on Highway 1 is another regular haunt of local birders. The grounds of Uniacke House are typical of the area, which supports a varied nesting population of songbirds. **Pileated Woodpecker, Yellowbellied Sapsucker, Eastern Phoebe, Yellowbellied Flycatcher, Solitary Vireo, Blackpoll and Wilson's Warblers, Northern Waterthrush and Rosebreasted Grosbeak** are all widespread, and the flowers attract **Rubythroated Hummingbird** in fall. Brooklyn Pond has **American Bittern, Wood and Ringnecked Ducks** among its breeding waterbirds, and a **Belted Kingfisher** is on hand to provide a bonus most visits.

The last place I'll mention is in way of an obituary. The unromantic-sounding Dartmouth Piggery just east of Dartmouth Hospital is no more. The swamp and bordering alders often attracted **Sora and Virginia Rail** in late fall and early winter when the resident **Ruffed Grouse** could be seen, but it was most famous for its flycatchers. Apart from the almost mundane **Western Kingbird**, this exotic locale turned up **Say's Phoebe, Fork-tailed and Scissortailed Flycatchers**. The swampy alders also provided cover for good numbers of warblers and sparrows in fall and early winter when groups of **Whitecrowned and Swamp Sparrows** joined the resident **Whitethroated and Song Sparrows**. Rarer visitors included **Northern Cardinal, Blackheaded Grosbeak, Rufous-sided Towhee and Field Sparrow**, and a number of **Indigo Bunting**. Warblers tended to leave quickly, but **Bluewinged and Prairie Warblers** stayed long enough to be seen. Icterids tended to be more accommodating, and the usual species were joined by **Brewer's and Yellowheaded Blackbird, and Dickcissel**. I may be a swine for saying so, but I regret the town's decision to replace the piggery with housing development.

THE CIRCUIT

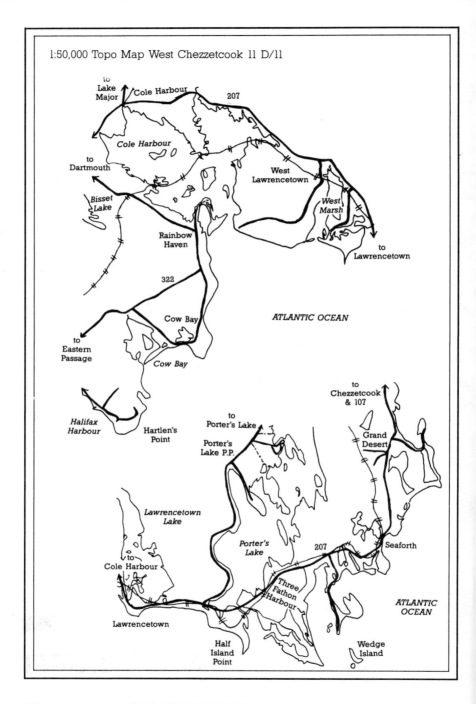

1:50,000 Topo Map West Chezzetcook 11 D/11

to
Lake
Major

Cole Harbour

207

Cole Harbour

to
Dartmouth

West
Lawrencetown

West
Marsh

to
Lawrencetown

Bisset
Lake

Rainbow
Haven

322

Cow Bay

ATLANTIC OCEAN

to
Eastern
Passage

Cow Bay

Halifax
Harbour

Hartlen's
Point

to
Porter's Lake

Porter's
Lake P.P.

to
Chezzetcook
& 107

Grand
Desert

Lawrencetown
Lake

Porter's
Lake

207

Seaforth

to
Cole Harbour

Lawrencetown

Three
Fathon
Harbour

ATLANTIC
OCEAN

Half
Island
Point

Wedge
Island

The coastline east of Dartmouth is a continuation of the Atlantic Coast region found from Yarmouth to Mahone Bay and interrupted by the granite barrens west of Halifax. The slates and quartzites produce ridges and valleys, and the submerging coast has created many drowned estuaries and headlands. Sand beaches and saltmarshes in the region support a very rich coastal and marine environment very popular with marsh and shorebirds, and as a result birders. This region is so well-known, in fact, that local birders have dubbed it simply "The Circuit".

It is accessible from several directions, but the usual approaches are from Dartmouth by way of Highway 322 through Eastern Passage and Cow Bay or Highway 207 by way of Cole Harbour. A combination of the two routes is possible except in winter when the Rainbow Haven link road may be closed. The varied mixture of forest, scrub, salt-marshes, sandy beaches, rocky windswept points and sheltered bays attracts more than their share of rarities year round. In spring northbound ducks and shorebirds are prominent before the summer invasion of the beaches reduces the nesting success of **Piping Plover** and other summer residents. The first returning shorebirds arrive in the first week of July and their numbers are high well into October. Marshbirds are also fairly common in late summer and fall. Loons, grebes and diving ducks take over in early winter, and then geese, and any lingering songbirds, provide the main attraction.

The first community reached along Highway 322 is Eastern Passage. Wintering **Common and Redthroated Loons** have been joined by stray **Arctic Loon** several times, but there are rarely many birds beyond the usual wintering alcids and gulls. Swirling flocks of **Snow Bunting** may contain a few **Lapland Longspur**, and there is a chance of finding **Sharptailed, Seaside and "Ipswich" Sparrows** among the usual lingering **Savannah Sparrows** until early December. Good numbers of **Rednecked Grebe** return to the area by mid April, and a **Mew Gull** has been seen in May when a **Warbling Vireo** provided the only unusual songbird reported. A **Mew Gull** has also spent the first part of the fall feeding around the harbour. A tropical hurricane was the source of a wreck of **Black Skimmers** in October 1968, and there are sometimes a few **Leach's and Wilson's Storm-petrels, and Dovekies** deposited here in late fall and early winter.

Just beyond is the road to the golf course and Hartlen's Point. This is an excellent place to watch for pelagics in spring and seaducks in fall, but almost any time of year will reveal good birds. I have been here on a very cold day in winter when the **Snow Bunt-ings** were sharing the beach with a few **Horned Lark and Lapland Longspur**. An odd

Harlequin, Dovekie or Thickbilled Murre is found on the water at this time, and a **Killdeer** may hang noisily around until late January. The first returning **Rednecked Phalarope** has been reported in early April, when parties of **20 Common Loon, 50 Rednecked Grebe and 30 Northern Gannet** appear. Counts of **3000 Common Eider** are not unusual at this time, and there may be a few **King Eider, Surf Scoter, Thickbilled Murre and Dovekie** for variety. **Whitewinged Scoter** are more often seen later in the spring migration in late May. **Marsh Wren** nests in the area and may be seen any time from mid May to early December.

The best time to visit is probably fall. The grassland of the golfcourse and the heath of the headland attract **Lesser Golden Plover and Buffbreasted Sandpiper**, and there are often **Red and Rednecked Phalaropes** offshore. Some of the shorebirds leave here very late as late October **Little Stint**, early November **Ruff** and late November **Baird's Sandpiper** records indicate. Up to **2500 Doublecrested Cormorant** have been counted flying by in long, ragged skeins in late October, shortly before **Northern Gannet** wing by at rates of **200-250** an hour. **King Eider** is a strong possibility at this time and into early winter when any wintering loons and grebes appear. Songbirds sometimes get stranded at the point for a few days. Some of the more interesting have been **Yellowbreasted Chat, 9 Brown Creeper** (there are no trees!), **Indigo Bunting, Sharptailed, Seaside and Claycolored Sparrows**. The first **Lapland Longspur** parties arrive late in September — this is one of the best places to see them.

You can walk along the shoreline to check out the waters of Cow Bay, but it is best to return to the main road at Eastern Passage and drive about 2 miles to the headland on the other shore. From here you can walk down to the beach and along the spit where **Common and Arctic Terns** may be seen any time from mid May to early December. **Roseate Tern** is a strong possibility in summer, but a mid July **Gullbilled Tern** has to be considered extralimital. **Tricolored Heron, Sora and Merlin** have appeared in early spring when **Rednecked Grebe** is common. By early May their numbers may be up to **160**, and the beaches can be scoured for a few northbound shorebirds, especially **Lesser Golden Plover**.

However, the fall is the best season to visit. Mid August brings a number of early **Hooded Merganser** and dabbling ducks near the causeway, and diving ducks soon follow. Huge numbers of **Greater Scaup, Common Goldeneye, Oldsquaw, Common Eider, Whitewinged, Surf and Black Scoters** can be seen by parking at the top of the hill above Cow Bay. **Canvasback and Ruddy Duck** have been noted in early November, and **Arctic Loon and King Eider** have been seen a few times in early winter. These birds often stay into the winter when a few **Purple Sandpiper** may be seen flying by. There are nearly always a few songbirds hanging around late with the wintering **American Tree and Savannah Sparrows**.

The marshes from Cole Harbour to Lawrencetown are now part of a Coastal Heritage Provincial Park system. Whether this will provide the protection they need is open to debate, but any protection is better than none for the sand dunes, saltmarshes, sand and cobble beaches included. Cole Harbour can be reached from Cow Bay by taking a left turn at Rainbow Haven, which provides an excellent view of the marshes opposite Conrad's Beach (see later). The road joins up with Highway 207 from Dartmouth just beyond Bissett Lake. Cole Harbour is a sprawling community alongside a saltwater inlet that has **4000+ Canada Geese** in winter. This flock has attracted occasional **Snow Geese** in fall, and even **2 Greater Whitefronted Geese** in mid November. **Great Horned**

Owl are sometimes flushed from woodlots, but the most interesting winter residents are **Sharptailed Sparrows** of the inland race. Large flocks of **Doublecrested Cormorant** can be seen flying by in April, but ducks are a minor feature compared to fall, although there has been a **Eurasian Wigeon** in spring. Very few songbirds have been noted, even in spring when the rarities include **Summer Tanager, Blue Grosbeak** and more often **Indigo Bunting**.

Canada Goose

RB
1987

Fall is an exciting time to visit, both for waterfowl and for shorebirds. The shorebirds arrive first, as early as mid July, and stay until mid October. Some of the larger counts have been **340 Semipalmated Plover, 150 Blackbellied Plover, 205 Lesser Golden Plover, 325 Shortbilled Dowitcher, 130 Least Sandpiper, 195 Whiterumped Sandpiper and 1000 Semipalmated Sandpiper**. Good numbers of **Ruddy Turnstone, Willet** — including a few western birds, **Greater and Lesser Yellowlegs** also stop here. Low tide will also reveal a few **Piping Plover, Killdeer, Whimbrel, Red Knot, Pectoral Sandpiper and Hudsonian Godwit** on the mudflats and small islands between the road and railway track bisecting the inlet. The peak migration takes place between August and September and has brought reports of **Baird's, Stilt and Western Sandpipers, Dunlin, Longbilled Dowitcher, Rednecked and Wilson's Phalaropes** and even an **American Avocet**.

Another fall feature is the build up of **Great Blue Heron** on the mudflats where as many as **60** gather at low tide until late September. Not surprisingly, these birds have brought in **Yellowcrowned Night Heron, Snowy and Cattle Egrets, Little Blue Heron and Least Bittern**. By October, the best time to visit is high tide when the first flocks of geese act as sentinels for shot-shy **Black Duck, Northern Pintail, Greenwinged and Bluewinged Teal**. A careful search may also reveal a **Ruddy Duck or Canvasback**. This is also one of the few localities where more than one **Forster's Tern** has been seen — a party of **6** arrived after a recent October storm. Songbirds can be seen in the small woodlots, but very few have been reported except a late September **Yellowbreasted**

Chat. However, Rosemary Eaton's feeder has had a number of rarer species. **Field, Chipping and Whitecrowned Sparrows** are quite regular among the **American Tree and Whitethroated Sparrows**, and there are usually **Northern Oriole, Dickcissel and Eastern Meadowlark** in the fields. **Claycolored and Lark Sparrows** are rare enough, but a **Greentailed Towhee** was certainly a bonus one year.

The next stop is West Lawrencetown which lies south of Highway 207 and can be reached by taking a short road less than a mile before the Conrad's Beach turnoff. This area is noted for its concentration of dabbling ducks, many of which can be seen from the main road by looking over West Marsh. As many as **1500 Canada Geese** may be flushed here from Cole Harbour, and good numbers of **Black Duck, Mallard, Northern Pintail, Greenwinged and Bluewinged Teal**, and somewhat fewer **Northern Shoveler and American Wigeon** are present in fall. Rarer visitors have included **Common Teal, Redhead, Lesser Scaup, Ruddy Duck and Hooded Merganser**.

The marshes are also very popular with **Yellowcrowned Night Heron, Great, Snowy and Cattle Egrets, Little Blue Heron, Glossy Ibis, American Coot and Virginia Rail**, and there has even been a May **Tricolored Heron** for good measure. Shorebirds are seen in fall, especially **Lesser Yellowlegs**, and **Stilt Sandpiper** is probably a regular visitor—although a mid August count of **26** here and at Lawrencetown has to be considered exceptional. **Common and Arctic Terns** nest in the area and sometimes attract **Black Tern**, but a June **Gullbilled Tern** was an obvious stray. Winter feeders keep a few **Mourning Dove, Blue Jay, Blackcapped and Boreal Chickadees, Redbreasted Nuthatch**, finches and sparrows around, and there is nearly always a **Belted Kingfisher** to be seen. Warblers are very common in the scrubby growth in spring when **Tree, Barn, Bank and Cliff Swallows** are quite common over the marsh.

The next stop is another goldmine for rarer birds. Conrad's Beach has long been a favoured nesting site for **Piping Plover** with family parties in early June, and it served as the southernmost breeding location for **Least Sandpiper** until Massachusetts came up with a nest in 1979. **Willet** are much more vocal in defence of their young and have the annoying habit of alerting everything on the marshes if you venture too close. This is not a problem in spring when **Lesser Golden and Blackbellied Plovers and Sanderling** provide evidence of northbound birds. There have even been a few **Whimbrel and Ruff** from late April and an even more surprising **Buffbreasted Sandpiper** which usually chooses a continental route north. April counts of **100 + Rednecked Grebe and 42 Great Cormorant** provide a commentary on spring movement of seabirds. Midsummer is given over to the vocal refrains of **Redwinged Blackbird and Sharptailed Sparrow**, and an occasional visit from postbreeding **Little Blue Heron**.

The best birding is certainly in fall when the beaches attract large numbers of most eastern shorebirds and a few regular westerners. Clouds of **Least and Semipalmated Sandpipers** swirl over the flats at low tide, especially if a **Merlin or Peregrine** is on the hunt, and counts of **100 Greater and 225 Lesser Yellowlegs** are higher than most other Atlantic sites. **800 Shortbilled Dowitcher** in early August is also a fair indication of a heavy early movement, and mid July has brought a **Wilson's Plover**. Rarities like **Baird's, Stilt and Western Sandpipers** are fairly regular, and **Wilson's Phalarope** is almost guaranteed each year. Most birds have left by late October, but a few **Blackbellied Plover, Red Knot and Dunlin** may decide to stay on for the Halifax East count. **Snowy Egret, Least Bittern and Sora** may appear any time in the late summer and early fall, but there are rarely many ducks, although **Hooded Merganser** have been noted in late August.

The commonest winter songbird is the **Snow Bunting**, but the cold winters and snow cover do not seem to deter a few **Whitethroated, Sharptailed and Seaside Sparrows** from overwintering in the dune grasses. There have also been reports of **Marsh Wren, Eastern Meadowlark and Field Sparrow**.

Lawrencetown Lake to the east often has ducks at high tide, as a count of **22 Bluewinged Teal** in late September and **Lesser Scaup** in mid November indicate. The lake is crossed by a roadbridge and a railway bridge, and it is worth walking along the old railway line towards the shore where it again meets the road. There are usually one or two **Osprey** nests, and ducks on the water. **Common Goldeneye, Bufflehead, American Wigeon and Gadwall** are regular, and the marshy areas attract occasional **Little Blue and Tricolored Herons. Sharptailed Sparrow** nest here in summer, and **Bald Eagles** are often seen in winter. You can climb to the headland to look for **Common Loon and Great Cormorant**, and offshore **Redthroated Loon, Rednecked, Horned** and sometimes **Piedbilled Grebes. Snowy Owls** are possible in winter.

Lawrencetown is a good place to walk along the marshes and sandflats to count birds and look for rarities. Typical maximum counts are **330 Semipalmated Plover, 135 Blackbellied Plover, 70 Ruddy Turnstone, 125 Lesser and 80 Greater Yellowlegs, 65 Willet, 350 Shortbilled Dowitcher, 140 Least and 425 Semipalmated Sandpipers, and 115 Sanderling**. Add in **Piping Plover, Whimbrel, Red Knot, Hudsonian Godwit, Dunlin, Spotted, Pectoral and Whiterumped Sandpipers**, and it is easy to see why this area is so well birded in fall. There is also a good chance of adding **Solitary, Baird's and Stilt Sandpipers, Longbilled Dowitcher, Ruff and Wilson's Phalarope**.

Stilt Sandpiper

Gulls and terns also like this area. **Ringbilled, Blackheaded and Bonaparte's Gulls** are quite common after most of the terns leave. The wisdom of checking out the flocks is indicated by the presence of an immature **Laughing Gull** in mid July, a **Forster's Tern** in mid November, and a **Mew Gull** in mid February. A few marshbirds can be expected to fly over from West Lawrencetown and Three Fathom Harbour, including **Little Blue Heron**, but like waterfowl they are rarely a major attraction here. The same applies to songbirds, although **Redwinged Blackbird** nest here, and there have been sightings of **Marsh Wren, Yellowthroated Vireo and Blue Grosbeak** away from the marshes.

The next section is known locally as Rocky Run and leads towards Half Island Point. **Common Redpoll, American Goldfinch, Purple Finch, Pine Siskin, Boreal Chickadee** and a selection of woodpeckers are regularly seen here. **Ruffed Grouse** can also be heard drumming in spring. The headland known as Half Island Point can be reached by following a rough road. **Greater Scaup** are common in winter, and there may be a **Dovekie, Common or Thickbilled Murre** riding the waves. **Gray Jay, Pine Grosbeak, Red and Whitewinged Crossbills, and Darkeyed Junco** winter here, and a **Common Raven** may occasionally loom large among the omnipresent **Common Crows**.

A real jewel of a saltmarsh is part of a private sanctuary located at nearby Three Fathom Harbour. The access road leads east over the railway tracks to a harbour and headland. The quaintly named Nirvana Pond has had breeding **Piedbilled Grebe, Common Moorhen and Ringnecked Duck**, and the rarities found here from spring to fall put many sites to shame. Where they all come from is a mystery since storms do not seem to be a factor. Summer vagrants have included **Pomarine Jaeger, Gullbilled, Royal and Least Terns, and Laughing Gull**. There must be a factor to turn larids on because the **Arctic Tern** colony always has a few **Black Tern**, and an October **Sooty Tern** and December **Forster's Tern** are unique for the region.

While strays are a major attraction, this is a major staging area for marshbirds, shorebirds and ducks. A number of **Blackcrowned and Yellowcrowned Night Herons** have appeared here, and both **Snowy Egret and Common Moorhen** are considered regular. **Great and Cattle Egrets** are less regular but can be looked for in late summer when **Little Blue and Tricolored Herons** have both been seen. There has even been a unique **"Great White" Heron** in May. Shorebirds don't take a back seat, with the parade of rarities topped by regular visits from as many as **6 Longbilled Dowitcher and Stilt Sandpiper**. Pride of place must go to an amazing **3+ Curlew Sandpiper** in mid October — this rarely happens even in Europe! **Wilson's Phalarope** find the marshy ponds attractive, and there are sometimes some **Rednecked Phalaropes** in the area in October.

Ducks are also plentiful here with **Gadwall, Northern Shoveler, American Wigeon, Wood Duck and Redhead** fairly regular, and **Eurasian Wigeon, Lesser Scaup, Ruddy Duck and Hooded Merganser** less frequent migrants. The offshore flocks are also worth checking for **King Eider**, and **40 Bufflehead** and sometimes a **Barrow's Goldeneye** winter with the **200 Common Goldeneye** in the area. **Redtailed and Roughlegged Hawks** are often seen in winter when falcons or **Northern Shrike** may turn up. A late **Turkey Vulture** around the Thanksgiving weekend and an overwintering **Varied Thrush** add an element of surprise after the marshbirds and shorebirds have left.

Causeway Road beyond Three Fathom Harbour is the access point to Wedge, or Fox, Island, where **Roseate Tern** breeds some summers. Seaducks and loons are common here in early winter. **Common Eider, Redbreasted Merganser** and all three scoters can be seen with a few **Common Loon** and on one occasion a **Harlequin**. The most conspicuous winter residents are parties of **Purple Sandpiper**, but there are always a few songbirds hanging around the fishing stores and lobster pots in winter when **Grasshopper, Sharptailed and Seaside Sparrows** have all been discovered. The most unusual vagrant was a mid October **Blue Grosbeak**, but **Eastern Meadowlark** is eminently possible in fall.

The short causeway beyond at Seaforth provides a good lookout point for seaducks, loons and grebes in the winter months. If birds can't be seen from the road, you can park and climb up the trail alongside the bluff to look down on them. There are **Common and Redthroated Loons, Horned and Rednecked Grebes, Common Eider, Oldsquaw, Whitewinged and Black Scoters** to be seen. **Bufflehead and Surf Scoter** are also regular, and **3 Eurasian Wigeon** in November and both **Arctic Loon and King Eider** on several occasions demonstrate the value of checking out the rafts and individual birds. A drake **Common Teal** has also appeared in mid May — a month after the passage of **1000 Doublecrested Cormorant and Northern Gannet. Shorteared Owl** are regularly found hunting along the headlands, and an immature **Broadwinged Hawk** has shown up in mid December, as has **Marsh Wren** — also in late April. Another excellent place along this coastline is at the community of Grand Desert where Highway 207 heads north for Chezzetcook. This area has produced a late fall-early winter crop of marshbirds, including several **Sora and Virginia Rail, Killdeer and Common Snipe. Little Blue Heron, Least Bittern, King and Clapper Rails** have also appeared here.

Other places to visit from this area

The outskirts of Dartmouth have a number of lakes, of which Bissett Lake is the closest to town. There have been nesting records of **Piedbilled Grebe** here and also a late November **Ruddy Duck**. Access is from Highway 207 off the Rainbow Haven road. More productive year round is the cottage-dotted Echo Lake-Porter's Lake region. **Bald Eagle and Osprey** both nest, and the lakeshores and marshes are quite productive in late spring and early fall when **Tricolored Heron and Common Moorhen** have been recorded. **American Coot** is more likely and may linger to the Christmas Count period when **Bluewinged and Greenwinged Teal** have been seen. The feeders attract a few strays such as **Dickcissel, Lark, Claycolored and Field Sparrows**, but most of the winter residents are lingering species like **Mourning Dove, Redbreasted Nuthatch, Marsh Wren, Northern Oriole and Chipping Sparrow**.

Beyond The Circuit, or an extension of it, is Chezzetcook Inlet which has a similar variety of birds as other sites. Up to **40 Willet** have been noted in late April, but shorebirds are really a fall feature. Typical numbers on a fall visit are **90 Semipalmated Plover, 250 Blackbellied Plover, 175 Lesser Yellowlegs, 350 Shortbilled Dowitcher, 500 Semipalmated Sandpiper and 200 Sanderling. Lesser Golden Plover and Willet** also appear in small numbers, and wandering marshbirds, including a late summer **Little Blue Heron** and more regular egrets, add variety. After the shorebirds have left, **Bald Eagle** is a winter speciality. These birds fly over the water and disturb flocks of **Black Duck, Black Scoter, Bufflehead** and occasional **Mallard** which winter here. I can always remember gingerly following Ian MacLaren as he strode purposefully over the early winter ice to confirm an identification. He was out and back before we got halfway! Nesting **Rusty Blackbird**, a July **Roughwinged Swallow** and a mid October **Marsh Wren** are all the coastal woods and marshes have produced to date.

Martinique Beach Game Sanctuary is a long sandspit at the entrance to Musquodoboit Harbour where I was lucky enough to see the only Atlantic **Zonetailed Hawk**. This area has the largest wintering flocks of **Canada Goose and Black Duck** in Atlantic Canada — about **5000 and 3000. 30+ Bufflehead** also winter, along with **Rednecked Grebe, Whitewinged Scoter and Northern Pintail**. A **Eurasian Wigeon** has appeared in November after which **Harlequin and Hooded Merganser** are also possible. **Bald**

Eagles often put the birds to flight, and there have been recent reports of a **Golden Eagle**. A flock of **Purple Sandpiper** winters on the spit, and may be joined by a few **Dunlin and Sanderling**. A late April **Tricolored Heron** was a recent addition to the sanctuary list.

Piping Plover nest on the sandspit, and marshbirds also use the area on migration, with **Snowy Egret and Gullbilled Tern** having appeared in early July. Counts of **200+ Red Knot and 250 Dunlin** are the highest along this shoreline, and the same number of **Shortbilled Dowitcher** also pass through early. Late July is also the time to look for **Whimbrel and Willet**, and there was a **Eurasian Whimbrel** one year in mid August. Martinique Beach was also the location that answered two questions: a fall "wreck" left **7 Manx Shearwater** dead on the beach, and this led to the discovery of their nest sites in Newfoundland; and the evidence of **Savannah/Ipswich Sparrow** interbreeding on the mainland helped relegate the Sable Islander from full species to subspecies or race status.

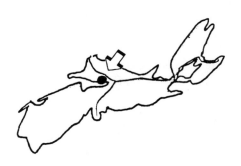

COBEQUID BAY

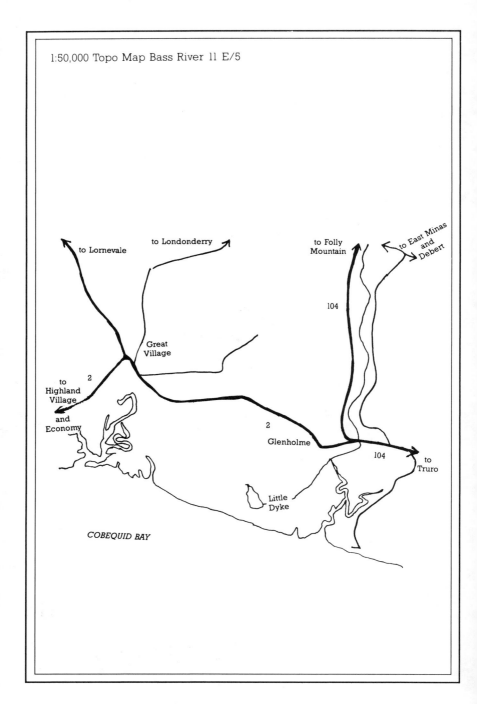

1:50,000 Topo Map Bass River 11 E/5

to Lornevale

to Londonderry

to Folly
Mountain

to East Minas
and
Debert

104

Great
Village

to
Highland
Village

2

and
Economy

2

Glenholme

104

to
Truro

Little
Dyke

COBEQUID BAY

Cobequid Bay is the continuation of Minas Basin east to Truro. The narrowing of the saltwater basin produces tidal bores similar to those in Moncton, New Brunswick and elsewhere along the Bay of Fundy. At low tide there are extensive mudflats, and the low sandstone shoreline on both sides of the bay is covered by glacial deposits which have been cleared for farming, although not to the extent shown in the similar Annapolis Valley. The forest cover is mainly mixed, although the Debert area has jack pine and heaths. Truro is the only large town in the area.

The Cobequid Mountains were once as high as the Canadian Rockies, but erosion has reduced them to less than 1,000 feet in height, although they do offer alpine skiing at Wentworth and sometimes very hazardous driving around Folly Lake. Most of the breeding birds in the mountains are boreal species, plus **Pileated Woodpecker** and a few summering **Hooded Merganser**, and a southern element was introduced by a midsummer **Blackcrowned Night Heron** at Lake Wentworth. However, the most productive birding is along the coast.

The best sites in the area are between 8 and 36 miles northwest of Truro on the Glooscap Trail. The first stop should be at Debert Wildlife Management Area — the site of some of the earliest recorded settlement in Canada. Paleo-Indians hunted migrating caribou around 9000 BC, and flints can still be found, although both Indians and caribou have long since disappeared. The sanctuary can be seen to the left of exit 13 on Highway 104. **Eurasian Wigeon and Greenbacked Heron** have provided some excitement in spring, but American ducks are the main attraction. **Wood Duck** have been encouraged to nest in special tree boxes, and the sanctuary also has breeding **Black Duck, Bluewinged Teal, American Wigeon and Ringnecked Duck**. Good numbers of most dabbling duck species and **Canada Goose** gather here in fall when **Snow Goose and Gadwall** are both possible.

The nearby dykelands provide good views of nesting **Bobolink** and have large numbers of **Lesser Golden Plover** in fall. Most of the shorebirds are found on the coast at Lower Debert, which lies a short distance to the left at the end of a minor road. **Whimbrel** are common into September, when there may be up to **5000 + Semipalmated Sandpiper, 850 Semipalmated Plover, 30 Red Knot, 25 Dunlin and 50 Least Sandpiper** along the shore. The farmlands have a number of resident **Gray Partridge and Ringnecked Pheasant**.

The next area is located west of the junction of Highways 104 and 2. The Glenholme-Great Village area is mainly farmland, but there is an excellent marsh just east of Great Village. Follow a road to the shore at Coupar's Pig Farm to where **Shorteared Owl and Sharptailed Sparrow** nest. **Gray Partridge** are also resident in the surrounding fields, but are hard to find. The best time to look is in late fall and winter when hunting **Rough-legged Hawks** may disturb the flocks. There are also **Ruffed Grouse and Ringnecked Pheasant** year-round, and as many as **40 Mourning Dove** have wintered at the pig farm. One very rare May visitor was a **Sandhill Crane**. Some of the highest fall shorebird counts in Cobequid Bay are at Highland Village where **45,000 Semipalmated Sandpiper, 500 Semipalmated Plover, 110 Blackbellied Plover and 200 Least Sandpiper** are regularly seen.

I recently discovered the secondgrowth woodlands at Portapique, but cottage development may destroy much of this habitat for nesting flycatchers, warblers and sparrows. **Tennessee, Magnolia and Nashville Warblers, Common Yellowthroat, American Redstart, Chipping, Whitethroated and Song Sparrow** were all on territory in this habitat.

A little further along the shore, Francis Spalding has carried on a birding tradition started by the Hennesseys. Economy Point marks the transition between Cobequid Bay and Minas Basin, and is also the boundary of the cleared land and coniferous forests. Economy is, therefore, a very good place to look for both farmland and boreal forest birds. **Spruce Grouse, Blackbacked Woodpecker and Mourning Warbler** are all widespread, and all but three of Nova Scotia's breeding warblers have been seen in the Economy area. Bass River has several pairs of **Barred Owl and Pileated Woodpecker**, and a rare **Redheaded Woodpecker** has been seen in late May. **Sharpshinned Hawk, American Kestrel, Eastern Kingbird, Eastern Wood-pewee and Rusty Blackbird** also nest in small numbers. **Ringnecked Pheasant and Gray Partridge** stray close to the roads between Bass River and Economy, and an evening visit will turn up a few territorial **American Woodcock. Redtailed Hawk** are also possible.

Spring can be quite interesting with a fair number of **Redthroated Loon and Surf Scoter** in early May and a few shorebirds. There have been as many as **110 Blackbellied Plover** in late May, so a Eurasian stray can eventually be expected, although a mid April **Upland Sandpiper** is the best shorebird so far. Mid April also produced a **Glossy Ibis** too late for a wintering **Gyrfalcon** to sample. **Doublecrested Cormorant and Whitewinged Scoter** both summer, and **Whitewinged, Surf and Black Scoters** are joined by **Common Eider** rafts from September to November. **Northern Shoveler** are possible in late September when the wintering **Bufflehead** arrive, and a **Thickbilled Murre** has been noted as early as mid October.

Shorebird counts are lower than other Minas Basin sites, but **500 Semipalmated Plover, 500 Blackbellied Plover, 120 Ruddy Turnstone, 30 Willet, 75 Whiterumped Sandpiper, 40 Dunlin, 200 Least Sandpiper, 2000 Semipalmated Sandpiper and 825 Sanderling** are a reasonable return in fall. There are also a few **Killdeer, Lesser Golden Plover, Greater and Lesser Yellowlegs, Red Knot, Pectoral Sandpiper and Shortbilled Dowitcher** on the beaches and shoreline fields in fall. Spring is less productive, but nesting **Killdeer** may appear as early as late March. Little Bass River is a good spot to stop in mid May to look among the **100+ Whitewinged Scoter** offshore for a few **Surf Scoter**.

Francis Spalding has combed the shoreline often enough to confirm that **Seaside Spar-**

row is a regular late September-early November migrant, and there have also been a late fall **Pine Warbler** and early winter **Brewer's Blackbird, Blackheaded Grosbeak and Grasshopper Sparrow**. The best winter bird is a recent turn of the year **Say's Phoebe**, and the top spring landbird migrant so far is a **Blackbilled Cuckoo**. Bass River has had at least two fall and winter visits from **Redheaded Woodpeckers**.

Other places to visit from this area

The southern shore of Cobequid Bay is very similar to the north shore and has the highest tides in the world — 52 feet in winter! Good numbers of **Ruffed Grouse, Gray Partridge and Ringnecked Pheasant** are resident on the farmlands, and **Black Duck, Greenwinged and Bluewinged Teal** attract hunters from as far away as Halifax in the fall. The marshes also attract nesting **American Bittern and Sora**, and there may have been **Yellow Rail** at Noel. Local lakes have nesting **Piedbilled Grebe and Ringnecked Duck**, and the droning of roding **American Woodcock** and drumming of courting **Common Snipe** are familiar sounds in spring and early summer. The major aerial predator is the **Redtailed Hawk**, a few of which stay to winter, when they may be joined by **Roughlegged Hawk, Northern Harrier and Shorteared Owl**.

The best shorebird habitat is at Noel Shore where large numbers gather at the mouth of a small river. Up to **15,000 Semipalmated Sandpiper** are present, and **Semipalmated and Blackbellied Plovers, and Willet** are also common. **Red Knot, Shortbilled Dowitcher and Dunlin** all appear in fair numbers both here and at Moose Cove where there may be **6650 Semipalmated Sandpiper**.

The Shubenacadie River flows into Cobequid Bay at Maitland. This is an excellent place for waterfowl of all kinds and for **Bald Eagle** which winter along the river as far as Shubenacadie — a count of 12 is not unusual. **Great Cormorant** fly well inland and there are often a few **Snow Geese** among the **Canada Goose** flocks. **Brant** are a possibility in spring, and both **Mallard and Northern Pintail** stay to nest. The Shubenacadie Wildlife Park just east of exit 10 on Highway 102 always attracts a few breeding **Wood Duck**, and I have also seen a **Gadwall** here that appeared to be wild.

Birds of prey are a feature of the area. Apart from the resident **Bald Eagles**, there are **Osprey** in summer and **Redtailed Hawk and Great Horned Owl** year round. A mid April **Turkey Vulture** and mid February **Boreal Owl** were a little more unusual. **Killdeer** now breed near Shubenacadie and **Sora** nest in the marshy areas near the coast. The farmlands and small woods have attracted several May **Roughwinged Swallow**, summering **Blackbilled Cuckoo**, and even a wintering **Varied Thrush**. Most of the commoner songbirds breed in the area, including **Boreal Chickadee, Veery, Rosebreasted and Pine Grosbeaks, Lincoln's Sparrow** and 19 of the warblers, including **Northern Parula, Tennessee, Blackthroated Blue, Chestnutsided, Mourning and Canada Warblers**. The nearby Stewiacke River has **Common Merganser** and a few **Spruce Grouse** in the Middle Stewiacke area.

Truro is an attractive town built on a plain and surrounding hillsides. Its varied habitats have been well studied and documented by Ross Baker (see appendix). The 405 hectares of Victoria Park in the centre of town offer some of the best birdwatching in any urban area. **Eastern Wood-pewee, Brown Creeper, Whitebreasted and Redbreasted Nuthatches, Winter Wren, Rubycrowned Kinglet and Blackburnian Warbler** are unusual additions to city bird songs. The streams also offer nesting sites for **Killdeer and Spotted Sandpiper** and food for summering **Greater Yellowlegs** and even a visiting **Glossy Ibis** in spring. There are also **Blackbilled Cuckoo, Blackbacked and Pileated Woodpeckers and Eastern Phoebe** nesting within city limits some years.

Most eastern warblers visit Victoria Park and many stay to breed, including **Magnolia, Blackthroated Blue and Mourning Warblers. Least, Alder and Olivesided Flycatchers, Gray Catbird and Red Crossbill** are other regular nesters. **Boreal Chickadee, Solitary Vireo, Northern Parula, Rosebreasted Grosbeak, Common Redpoll, Indigo Bunting and Vesper Sparrow** have also stayed long enough in summer to suggest breeding has at least been attempted. Winter residents may include a few parties of **Bohemian Waxwing** (there are teacher's training, bible and agricultural colleges to support my student theory!), and some **Brownheaded Cowbird and Evening Grosbeak** at feeders. **Broadwinged Hawk** sometimes use Bible Hill as a marker in spring, and May usually brings **Winter Wren, Cape May Warbler, Whitecrowned and Lincoln's Sparrows**. Fall boasts good numbers of **Rubythroated Hummingbird, Blue Jay and Cedar Waxwing**, with **Yellowbreasted Chat and Rufous-sided Towhee** sometimes thrown in for good measure.

A little beyond Economy is the Five Islands area which is most closely connected with the Glooscap saga. The provincial park is an excellent spot from which to explore the coastline and is close to Parrsboro with its amethysts. All three scoters are common in May and a **Saw-whet Owl** has been seen in the park in late May. A small group of **Bufflehead** spend the first part of winter at Parrsboro, appearing again in April-early May, and other diving ducks may also arrive in November, especially **Greater Scaup.** **Hooded Merganser** almost certainly breed in the area, and the local ponds have **Wood and Ringnecked Ducks**. The Athol cattail marsh has good numbers of both **Common Grackle and Redwinged Blackbird**, and there are also **Gray Catbird** nests in the area. I also flushed a stray **Marsh Wren** from the cattails and saw several **Common Nighthawks** along the minor roads south of Maccan.

The Nova Scotia Bird Society has recently signed a lease for the protection of Spencer's Island, which has been carefully monitored by the Parrsboro-based Environmental Protection in Cumberland South (EPICS) group. **Great Blue Heron, Doublecrested Cormorant, Common Eider, Black Guillemot, Great Blackbacked and Herring Gulls** nest on the island. **Black Guillemots** are rare in the area, so protection of their sheer nesting cliffs is important here. The remainder of the Cumberland County shore has little to offer, although **Eastern Bluebird** may nest at Advocate and Cape Chignecto. **Snowy Owls** are fairly regular in winter, and the coniferous forests of the inland Chignecto Game Sanctuary support large numbers of moose and boreal birds, including **Spruce Grouse, Blackbacked and Threetoed Woodpeckers**.

AMHERST POINT

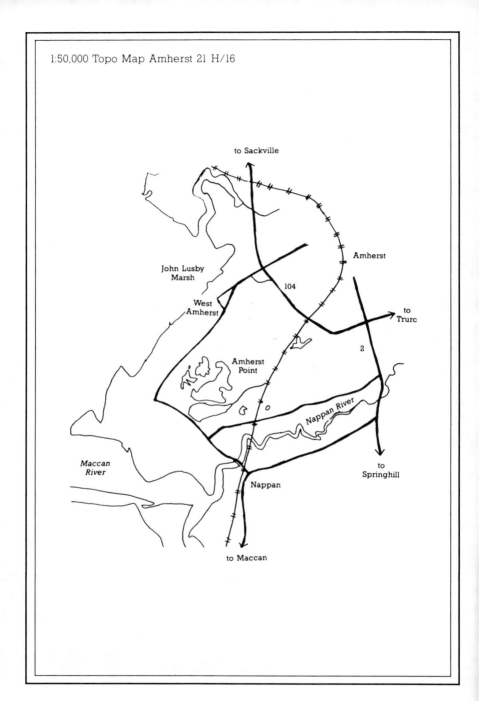

1:50,000 Topo Map Amherst 21 H/16

to Sackville

John Lusby
Marsh

Amherst

104

West
Amherst

to
Trurc

2

Amherst
Point

Nappan River

Maccan
River

to
Springhill

Nappan

to Maccan

■

The Isthmus of Chignecto occupies an area once flooded each year by the Fundy tides. Acadian farmers built dykes and controlled the saltwater flow, only occasionally allowing flooding to replenish the marine silts where they grew and cut their "marsh hay". The local name of the Tantramar Marshes comes from the old French "tintamarre" which described the noise made by thousands of wild ducks and geese. The older name has been restored in the National Wildlife Refuges and other wetland areas jointly managed by two levels of government and Ducks Unlimited Canada.

Ducks and geese are still the most important bird groups found here, but the area also supports a breeding population of marshbirds, raptors and songbirds unequalled anywhere else in Nova Scotia. Shorebirds are an additional fall attraction, and the winter months can also be very productive. Many of the birds fly to and from New Brunswick depending on the state of the tide and hunting pressure, so this is truly a Border Region which is the name used in much of the literature.

The best-known, and still arguably the best, birding site is Amherst Point Chignecto Migratory Bird Sanctuary, which still tops the provincial list in terms of breeding and migratory waterfowl and marshbirds. It lies just over 2 miles southwest of Amherst and covers about 3 sq. miles between the Nappan road, the main railway line and the Trans-Canada Highway. The southern boundary is the Amherst Ridge which dips here to form a silt bar. Many of the ponds are sinkholes caused by evaporation of saltwater, and water levels are now carefully controlled by dykes and sluice gates. Spring tides previously replenished the water supply and low levels of water in fall made the area very attractive to **Canada Goose and Brant**. Present management practices favour dabbling and diving ducks, both of which stay to breed in good numbers. The largest pond was drained in 1987 but will again be waterlogged in the 1990s. Each pond goes through this cycle every decade.

The best way to describe Amherst Point is to take the various bird groups separately and include any preferences for specific areas within the sanctuary. **Doublecrested Cormorant** is possible here and **Common Loon and Horned Grebe** are occasional winter and spring visitors, but the only regular member of this group is the **Piedbilled Grebe**. Amherst Point is a provincial stronghold of this species which nests on the large ponds, and less frequently on the other ponds. The distinctive courting song is a familiar sound in spring and early summer, but young birds are harder to find. There are as many as **15 pairs** here, and a total of **200** in fall indicates how successful they are.

Brant no longer appear in any numbers and **Snow Goose** is a rarity, but flocks of **Canada Geese** may spiral in from nearby Lusby Marsh where they usually feed. Dabbling ducks are always abundant, with feeding and resting parties on and around all the ponds. The small pond to the northwest, known as The Cove, sometimes has high numbers of **Black Duck, Northern Pintail and Bluewinged Teal**, together with a few **Mallard, Gadwall, American Wigeon, Northern Shoveler and Wood Duck**. Some breed here, but most choose the marshy area on the east of the large pond or the islands of the south pond. **Mallard** were released here in the 1950s, but they are now a threat to the **Black Duck** which may reach **500** in mid April and **250+** in fall. **American Wigeon** are the real story with **500+** in fall—birds stay into November.

Diving ducks are definitely increasing, and the trend has brought some new breeding species. **Ringnecked Duck** remain the commonest species with many family groups found on the two large ponds from mid June to early August. They tend to stage on the northeast pond where **100** can be counted in fall. The first provincial breeding records of both **Redhead and Ruddy Duck** occurred here, and both are now established on the south pond. **Common Goldeneye** return to the ponds in late September and are joined by regular **Bufflehead, Lesser Scaup and Redbreasted Merganser**. A few **Greater Scaup, Barrow's Goldeneye, Whitewinged and Black Scoters, Common and Hooded Mergansers** join them in late fall, and there is a good chance **Canvasback** may eventually discover the ponds.

Marshbirds are also common, with as many as **40 Great Blue Heron and 10 American Bittern** counted in late summer and early fall and a very varied selection of species in spring and summer. **Blackcrowned Night Heron** prefer the wooded area by the northwest pond, where **Greenbacked Heron** is also regular, but the **Great Egret and Little Blue Heron** visits are usually around the two large ponds, where **White and Glossy Ibis** have also been found. The bordering marshes are extremely popular with **American Coot** which are increasing, both as breeders and as early winter residents— more than **200** have been counted in late October and a few may linger into December before the ponds freeze. A few **Common Moorhen** now nest, but like the breeding **Sora and Virginia Rails** they are often hard to find. This is even more true of the secretive **Yellow Rail** which may be regular—my only Atlantic Canada sighting was in early fall. **Least Bittern, Cattle Egret and King Rail** have also appeared in summer.

Shorebirds appear in small numbers in spring, but they are a major feature in fall when numbers can be very high. **Lesser Golden Plover** start to appear in the fields in mid August, but the high counts of **700** are usually in September and early October when as many as **50 Killdeer** may join them. Other plovers are less often seen, but **Common Snipe** certainly are. Many birds breed and these numbers are augmented by migrants to over **500** in fall. Many birds feed in the northwestern pond where lower water levels and muddy fringes attract **500 Lesser Yellowlegs and 100+ Shortbilled Dowitcher** early and **50 Greater Yellowlegs and 180 Pectoral Sandpiper** late in fall. **Least and Semipalmated Sandpipers** can be found along any lake margin from July to mid September, but most of the late-arriving **100 Dunlin and 50 Whiterumped Sandpiper** feed along the dykes and on mud islands on the two large ponds. Several rarer species have been recorded, including a few **Hudsonian Godwit, Stilt Sandpiper and Wilson's Phalarope**. A careful check may also reveal a summer **Ruff** or mid fall **Longbilled Dowitcher**.

A few pairs of **Osprey** summer and have tried to build a nest on the power pole in the middle of the large pond—I have spent many hours "willing" one persistent bird to succeed but it never did! However, a visit in 1988 indicated the lesson had been learned, although the pond had been drained! **Redtailed and Sharpshinned Hawks, American Kestrel, Great Horned and Barred Owls** nest, and there have been fall sightings of **Northern Goshawk, Cooper's Hawk, Peregrine and Gyrfalcon**. The latter is fairly regular and I found a killing post with the remains of a coot one November. The usual wintering birds are **Redtailed and Roughlegged Hawks**, but a **Northern Harrier** sometimes stays and there may be **Shorteared Owls** on the marshes and **Merlin** in the woods. **Gray Partridge** formerly bred, but **Ruffed Grouse and Ringnecked Pheasant** are now the only likely gamebirds year round.

The woods are quite varied and attract a large summer population of both boreal and hardwood species. The woods to the north of the sanctuary, and especially the conifers between the northeast and large ponds, have **Common Raven, Gray Jay, Boreal Chickadee, Redbreasted Nuthatch, Brown Creeper, Goldencrowned and Rubycrowned Kinglets** and a few nesting **Blackbacked Woodpeckers**. These birds are joined by boreal finches in winter when a **Threetoed Woodpecker** is a definite possibility. Most warblers found in Nova Scotia nest here and are spread throughout the sanctuary. **Northern Parula, Tennessee, Nashville, Cape May, Chestnutsided, Blackburnian, Baybreasted and Canada Warblers** are among the better species, and **Philadelphia Vireo** is very likely among the much commoner **Redeyed and Solitary Vireos**. **Gray Catbird** is also regular and there are sometimes rarities like **Brown Thrasher and House Wren** on migration.

Eastern Kingbird and Alder Flycatcher share out the woods and secondgrowth, and there are always a few **Least and Olivesided Flycatchers, and Eastern Wood-pewee**. The path below the houses along the north edge of the sanctuary may also turn up an **Eastern Phoebe**. Thrushes and sparrows are extremely common in the woods, and I have heard the unmistakable song of a **Carolina Wren** here. **Redbreasted Nuthatch, Rubycrowned Kinglet and Yellowrumped Warbler** often stay into early winter, when flocks of **Darkeyed Junco and American Tree Sparrow** may be joined by **Rufous-sided Towhee, Chipping and Claycolored Sparrows**.

The marshes have a good number of nesting **Redwinged Blackbird** and I have also seen **Common Grackle** with young in summer, but the fields provide most of the nonforest songbirds in summer and winter. The song of the **Bobolink** is a tonic on summer visits, when flocks of **Barn, Tree and Bank Swallows** are augmented by the local **Cliff Swallows and Purple Martins** from nearby Amherst. Numbers in late summer can be staggering — as many as **100,000** birds have been counted on the wires. **Savannah, Swamp and Song Sparrows** are common nesters, and there are a few **Sharptailed Sparrow** to look out for in the wetter fields and marshes. **Eastern Bluebird and Loggerhead Shrike** used to nest here and may occasionally be seen in spring, but **Northern Shrike** is the more likely winter visitor at local feeders and perched on secondgrowth watching the flocks of **Snow Bunting and Lapland Longspur** in the fields.

While Amherst Point is composed of both salt and freshwater marshes and ponds, John Lusby Marsh on the other side of West Amherst is a saltmarsh bordering the tidal river. **Canada Goose** is the dominant species here with as many as **2000** on the marshes and fields in spring and fall. **Snow Geese** are regular among the flocks. Spring is the best time to visit for the geese and for the rarer dabbling ducks. **Black Duck, Northern Pintail and Greenwinged Teal** appear in mid April, and they are joined by **Bluewinged Teal** later in the month. From then to early June, there are always a few **Mallard, Gad-**

wall, **American Wigeon and Northern Shoveler** to draw your attention, and this is the only place where you can legitimately hope to see both **Eurasian Wigeon and Common Teal** on a regular basis.

By mid June all but the nesting pairs of ducks, which have included **Ruddy Duck**, have left the marsh, but **Blackcrowned Night Heron** and an occasional **Glossy Ibis** are possible in summer. **Blackbellied Plover, Ruddy Turnstone and Lesser Yellowlegs** often remain, and the bordering woods have all the usual warblers, plus **Blackbacked Woodpecker**. Parties of hirundines combing the marsh for insects may include **Roughwinged Swallow and Purple Martin**.

The marsh livens up again in late July when the shorebirds take it over. Over **100,000 Semipalmated Sandpiper** scurry across the flats at low tide and roost here. Counts of other species are just as impressive with **400 Semipalmated Plover, 300 Lesser Yellowlegs, 1000 Shortbilled Dowitcher, 55 Red Knot, 300 Least Sandpiper and 70 Hudsonian Godwit**. There have also been visits from **Willet, Ruff, Stilt Sandpiper, Longbilled Dowitcher, Wilson's and Rednecked Phalaropes**.

By September, most of the shorebirds have moved south and the ducks take over the marshes. Up to **300 Black Duck, 80 Northern Pintail, 500 American Wigeon, 140 Greenwinged and 50 Bluewinged Teal** feed on the flats. **Mallard, Gadwall, Northern Shoveler, Lesser Scaup and Ruddy Duck** are also fairly regular. **Yellowcrowned Night Heron and Snowy Egret** have been recorded in early fall when a **Yellow Rail** is possible, but **Common Moorhen, Sora and Virginia Rail** are more likely. Hunting is allowed on the marshes in October, so it is usually better to visit Amherst Point at this time since hunting is not permitted there and the birds feel safe. Visits in late fall and early winter are much less productive, but **Canada Goose, Black Duck, Common Merganser, Redtailed Hawk, Pileated Woodpecker, Horned Lark, Brown Creeper, Common Redpoll, American Tree and Song Sparrows, and Snow Bunting** can usually be found. Early winter **Gyrfalcon and Peregrine** scatter the ducks and shorebirds, but the usual wintering species are **Roughlegged Hawk and Northern Harrier**. There are also a few **Northern Shrike** in the area most winters.

Other places to visit from this site

Just south of Amherst Point, the Maccan road leads to another area of marshes managed by Ducks Unlimited Canada. Reached by driving along Highway 302 past Maccan, the shallow freshwater ponds and marshes are located either side of the tidal Maccan River. The eastern pond less than a mile past the community has fewer waterbirds, but it is an excellent place to look for warblers in spring. The larger western pond attracts dabbling ducks, **Sora** and a sprinkling of vagrant herons and egrets. **Little Blue Heron** is regular in spring and **Great, Snowy and Cattle Egrets** have all been recorded in recent years. The marshes are patrolled by **Northern Harrier and Shorteared Owl** in summer and fall, after which a few **Roughlegged and Redtailed Hawks, and Snowy Owl** may take over. Mid summer reports of **Cooper's Hawk** are worth checking out. **Killdeer and Gray Partridge** nest in the fields between here and Nappan where **Cliff Swallows** are very common. I have also seen a **Hoary Redpoll** in winter.

The adjoining waters of the Cumberland Basin are best checked from the New Brunswick side, but a road from Minudie offers a view that may include **500 Surf Scoter, 50+ Common Eider** and a few **Black Scoter** in spring. If hunting is a problem in fall, **Canada Geese** fly onto the basin where they may attract a few **Brant. Semipalmated**

Plover are the commonest shorebirds apart from the omnipresent **Semipalmated Sandpiper**, but most commoner species can be expected. **Redtailed Hawks** feed over the saltmarshes in fall but rarely winter.

The town of Amherst is famous for its three or four nesting colonies of **Purple Martin** which arrive in late April or early May to occupy their traditional sites. Birds can be seen flying over the town in summer, and there are nearly **100 young** raised before the birds leave in early September. The airways are shared with groups of chittering **Chimney Swift** and buzzing **Common Nighthawk. Barn Owl and Eastern Bluebird** have been rare spring visitors, and there are several **Pileated Woodpecker** nesting close to town. Eddy Marsh north of Lusby Marsh has breeding **Black Tern, Sora and Virginia Rail**, and West Amherst has had **Upland Sandpiper** in its fields in fall when there often large flocks of **Lesser Golden Plover**. Fall has also produced a mid October **Blackheaded Grosbeak**.

Winter is a good time to visit Amherst. There are usually a few **Whitebreasted and Redbreasted Nuthatches** sharing the feeders with **Blackcapped Chickadees**. The berry bushes attract good numbers of **Bohemian Waxwing and Pine Grosbeak** and the occasional **Northern Mockingbird and Song Sparrow**. Large flocks of **Snow Bunting** swirl over the fields and there are usually a few **Horned Lark and Lapland Longspur** in tow. **American Tree Sparrow and Darkeyed Junco** scour the weeds for food, and their flocks should be checked for **Dickcissel** and any lingering warblers or sparrows. A late **Pine Warbler** probably regretted its decision to winter, but **Yellowrumped Warbler, Whitecrowned and Chipping Sparrows** are better candidates for survival if they can avoid the wintering hawks and local cats.

Wood Duck

Missaguash Marsh, northeast of Amherst and reached by taking a red dirt road opposite the Biggs Drive turnoff in East Amherst, is part of the huge tidal complex and covers an area of 14 sq. miles, of which 80% is a floating sedge bog and lakes and 20% is cattail marsh. The carex bog has nesting **Black and Ringnecked Ducks**, while the cattail marsh harbours a variety of dabbling ducks, herons and rails. **Greenwinged and Bluewinged Teal, and Northern Pintail** are common in summer, when **Mallard, American Wigeon and Northern Shoveler** also have extra mouths to feed. **American Bittern and Common Snipe** are common in the area, and this is one of the few areas where **Wood Duck** regularly breed — it's not unusual to see **35** drake **Wood Duck** taking it easy here in late summer while the ducklings are taught the rudiments of survival. This can be confusing as the gene pool has been augmented by hybridization with both **Bluewinged and Greenwinged Teal**. The large **Sora** population is at times augmented by a few **Virginia Rails**, and occasional **Least Bitterns and Yellow Rails**.

This area deserves more attention since it has also had nesting **Blackcrowned Night Heron, Gadwall, American Coot, Common Moorhen and Black Tern**, as well as small colonies of **Marsh and Sedge Wrens** — which take possession of the two habitats they are named for but cannot be guaranteed. **Broadwinged Hawk** nest in the area, as do **Osprey**, and there have been spring visits from **Bald Eagle and Peregrine**. Shorebirds are typical of the region, with the mudflats having large numbers of **Semipalmated Sandpiper** and a few **Semipalmated and Blackbellied Plovers, Ruddy Turnstone, Greater and Lesser Yellowlegs, Least and Whiterumped Sandpipers** in fall. Mixed flocks of **Common Grackle, Redwinged Blackbird and Brownheaded Cowbird** might be checked for **Bobolink, Rusty** and maybe even **Brewer's Blackbird**. These disperse in winter when as many as **3500 Snow Bunting** spread out over the marshes and fields.

This is a good time to look for the many **Roughlegged Hawks** staking out territories around abandoned barns and disputing possession with any remaining **Northern Harrier or Shorteared Owl** or one of the rarer **Snowy Owls**. The adjoining fields were utilized by Atlantic Canada's first **Eurasian Kestrel** in the first half of 1988. The bird ranged from Minudie to Missaguash, crossing Chignecto Bay with ease while birders frantically scrambled into cars to make the long drive around. I was fortunate as the bird came to me in early June.

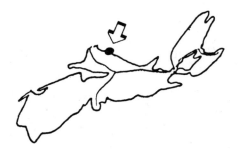

NORTHUMBERLAND STRAIT

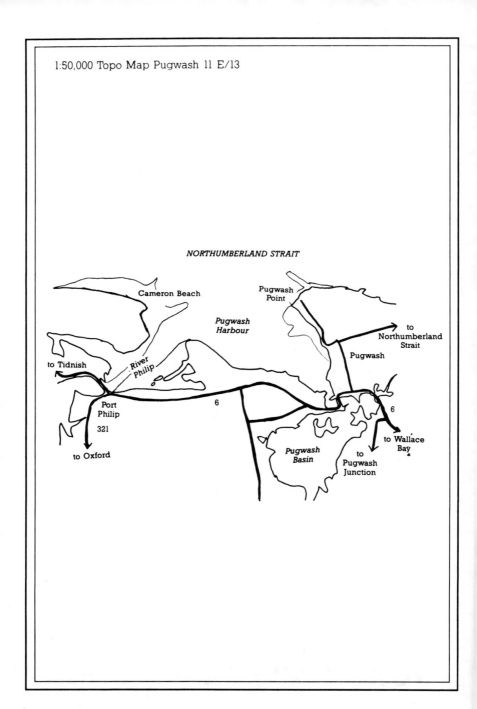

1:50,000 Topo Map Pugwash 11 E/13

NORTHUMBERLAND STRAIT

Cameron Beach

Pugwash
Point

Pugwash
Harbour

to Northumberland
Strait

to Tidnish

Pugwash

River
Philip

6

Port
Philip

6

321

to Wallace
Bay

to Oxford

Pugwash
Basin

to
Pugwash
Junction

The region east of Amherst is very popular with local residents who take advantage of the many beaches to enjoy bathing in waters that are 5°C warmer than those of other parts of the Gulf of Saint Lawrence. Several beaches are private, so permission to explore them and adjoining saltmarshes should be sought in advance whenever possible. However, most cottage-owners have left by the time the main attraction — waterfowl — arrive. The best section is found between River Philip and Tatamagouche and includes two bird sanctuaries.

The first area reached on the Sunrise Trail — Highway 6 — is the estuary of River Philip just west of Pugwash. Heather Beach off Highway 366 has had as many as **1000 Bank Swallow** on the sands in late August, but the main attractions are the large flocks of blackbirds gathering here in fall. Early flocks are quite likely to contain a few **Bobolink and Eastern Meadowlark**, but it is in the winter months when the fields are carpeted with **thousands** of the commoner species that you should look for **Brewer's Blackbird and Western Meadowlark** — both of which are appearing in Atlantic Canada on a more or less regular basis. **Dickcissel and Rufous-sided Towhee** have both reported from nearby River Philip in late fall. The road into River Philip often has **Gray Jay and Boreal Chickadee** in its small woodlots.

The open waters of Port Philip are probably the best place in the region to see **Redthroated Loon, Rednecked and Horned Grebes** at close range. These birds fish just below the old bridge and are present from late fall to early spring. Large numbers of **Canada Geese** also gather here through the winter and may be found either side of the road. As many as **500 Greater Scaup** are not unusual, especially inside the roadbridge, and they also remain for the winter with a few **Common and Redbreasted Mergansers**. **Bufflehead and Barrow's Goldeneye** are much less likely to be seen.

Early April sees a reduction in the number of **Greater Scaup**, but there may sometimes be a **Redhead and Lesser Scaup** or two with them. On the other hand, as many as **1400 Redbreasted and 210 Common Mergansers** have been counted at this time. Dabbling ducks prefer the saltflats and marshes at low tide — most are **Black Duck, Northern Pintail and Greenwinged Teal**. A spring visit may turn up a **Gadwall** among the small groups of **American Wigeon**, and **Brant** are finally returning after a long absence. Fall has somewhat higher numbers but less variety. A lingering **Glaucous Gull** may stay into April with the growing flock of **Ringbilled Gull**, but **Blackheaded Gull** is more likely to appear with the first **Common and Arctic Terns** of the summer.

The holiday resort of Pugwash 5 miles to the east has one of the best deepwater harbours in Nova Scotia. This is an excellent place to visit in winter when the overwintering ducks include **Barrow's Goldeneye**. This is, in fact, one of their few regular wintering sites in the province and there may be as many as **10**. The commonest diving ducks are **Common Goldeneye**, which may exceed **400** in late March, **Common Merganser and Oldsquaw**, but **Ringnecked Duck** can be found well into December. **Horned Grebe** visit the harbour, although numbers do not approach anything like the numbers found at Port Philip. The best viewpoint is at Pugwash Point which can be reached by driving straight in town after the bridge instead of taking Highway 6 east.

The next stop is the result of a recent decision to extend the number of national wildlife areas to the Northumberland Strait shore. The resulting Wallace Bay National Wildlife Area has attracted geese and ducks in great numbers and is rapidly rivalling Amherst Point in terms of numbers and potential breeding species. **Redhead** has already nested, and **Northern Shoveler, Lesser Scaup and Hooded Merganser** have checked the area out in spring and fall. As many as **85 Great Blue Heron and 8 Sora** in late August suggest that marshbirds find it attractive, too, but a summering immature **Greater Flamingo** obviously had a few things to learn.

Hudsonian Godwit

Shorebirds are well aware of the benefits offered by the management protection and the food available on the marshes. **Hudsonian Godwit** are regular visitors in July and August, and **Lesser Golden Plover and Dunlin** join the usual fall migrants. Fall visits have turned up large numbers of dabbling ducks, including **Mallard, Gadwall, American Wigeon and Bluewinged Teal**, in late August, when there may also be the first of the **Canada Geese** which peak at **1000+** in mid October. As many as **500 Ringbilled Gull** and a few **Bonaparte's Gull** gather here by late August, and it is often easy to pick out a **Blackheaded Gull** in later flocks. **Northern Harrier and Osprey** both stay late, but few raptors overwinter. The first **Lapland Longspur** arrive in September and take up residence with **Horned Lark, Snow Bunting** and a few hardy (or tardy) sparrows.

The Malagash Peninsula can be driven by means of a loop road to the left off the Sunrise Trail. The point is a good place to look for large numbers of **Greater Scaup** in early November, while the Tatamagouche Bay marshes are popular with shorebirds. The inner marshes just south of Malagash have had a successful nesting by **Common Moorhen** — three young being raised by mid August, and **Virginia Rail** have been heard calling in late May. The most visible birds are the fall parties of shorebirds, noted more for variety than numbers. **Blackbellied Plover and Semipalmated Sandpiper** are the commonest species out to Malagash Point, but counts of **30 Killdeer, 30 Lesser Golden Plover, 50 Willet, 50+ Greater Yellowlegs, 80 Red Knot and 60 Least Sandpiper** show potential for more. The flocks of **Whimbrel** in August have also brought in a **Marbled Godwit**.

Tatamagouche is certainly worth a visit in spring when good numbers of **Bluewinged Teal and Redbreasted Merganser** can be found. Shorebirds are also well represented with parties of **Blackbellied Plover, Willet and Greater Yellowlegs** very conspicuous in May. **Semipalmated Plover** may have nested at nearby Sand Point, which has also had both **Whimbrel and Marbled Godwit** two years in a row. The recently-created Ducks Unlimited marsh and pond had several **Ringnecked Duck**, a chugging **American Bittern** and two newly-hatched **Piedbilled Grebe** young on my mid-June visit. A **Bluewinged Teal** drake had a **Northern Shoveler** date for company. Passerines are common on spring migration with good counts of **Rubythroated Hummingbird, Least Flycatcher, Blackburnian and Chestnutsided Warblers, and Bobolink**. This is also a coastline well known for its birds of prey. **Osprey** use Cape John and Malagash Point as landmarks on the way north, and both **Golden Eagle and Redshouldered Hawk** have been reported in spring. The commonest breeding species is the **American Kestrel**. Fall offers a similar selection of species to those found elsewhere in Tatamagouche Bay.

The southern shore of Tatamagouche Bay has also received protection as the Brule Point Game Sanctuary. These marshes provide good habitat for migrant shorebirds. **Whimbrel** are regular as early as mid July, and small numbers of **Willet, Shortbilled Dowitcher and Least Sandpiper** feed here later in the month. **Semipalmated Plover** have nested and I also saw small numbers of **Bonaparte's Gull** and migrant **Blackbellied Plover, Semipalmated Sandpiper and Black Tern** on a mid-June visit. Up to **50 Ruddy Turnstone** can be expected at any time between late July and mid September. Spring migrants have included **Glossy Ibis and Rufous-sided Towhee**, while a fall visit is likely to turn up a **Snowy Egret** among the feeding **Great Blue Herons**.

A little further east, River John has had as many as **300 Common Merganser** in early November, and Semple Creek attracts **Canada Geese and Brant** in spring when **Great Blue Heron** sometimes take to flight as the first of the **Northern Harriers** glide by. The best birding is along the inner shoreline of Cape John. Amet Island — about 3 miles to the west of the Cape — has a sandbar which has harbour seals and a nesting colony of **Doublecrested Cormorant**. Mudflats, sandbars and saltmarshes also mean good shorebird habitats in fall. **Willet, Spotted Sandpiper**, and probably **Semipalmated Plover** nest close to the **Ringbilled Gull and Common Tern** colony, while the **Sharptailed Sparrows** have a hard time matching the melodies of **Bobolink** along the saltmarshes.

other places to visit from this area

Instead of taking the Sunrise Trail directly to Port Philip, a detour along Highway 366 by way of Tidnish is certainly in order. The waters of Baie Verte are very attractive to waterfowl as fall visits have clearly shown. The first **Common Loons** may appear inshore in mid September when a marauding **Parasitic Jaeger** and a western **Willet** offered variations on the 'white flash in the wing' routine, but the week before sees up to **250 Surf Scoter** on the water. As many as **45 Common Loon** stage here with a few **Redthroated Loon**, but the commonest members of this group are somewhat smaller. By late October as many as **55 Horned Grebe** have taken up winter residence, but they are upstaged by over **200 Rednecked Grebe**. Numbers of both species from Tidnish to Pugwash often exceed **250** from early October, and the peak counts may be much higher. Late pelagics like **Northern Gannet** pass close by from the Gulf of St. Lawrence.

The commonest bird is the **Redbreasted Merganser** which may total **1200** in November. **Brant** are more regular in May when they may be seen with a wandering **Great or Snowy Egret**, but a few appear with the influx of **Canada Geese** in fall. Ducks are less varied than in nearby managed areas, but one or two **Barrow's Goldeneye and Ruddy Duck** do appear on Baie Verte. Gulls are quite common, with **125 Bonaparte's Gull** a good count in mid October. A number of **Eastern Kingbirds** have taken a fancy to the fields by Northport, and a few stray songbirds appear in fall—the most notable being a mid September **Lark Sparrow**.

The section of coastline southeast of Cape John does not appear to have the same variety of birds as that to the north, but a visit to Caribou Island may be worthwhile. A gravel road leads off the Sunrise Trail at Caribou River and joins up with a road leading west from the Prince Edward Island ferry dock at Caribou. The nesting raptors on this peninsula are **Osprey**, which return to their nests by early May. and **Bald Eagle**, but visits from **Golden Eagle and Peregrine** seem to be increasing. Small numbers of **Black Scoter** arrive in May, but little is known of the breeding birds, although a late May **Vesper Sparrow** and some mid July **Roughwinged Swallows** suggest a summer visit is not going to be a total washout.

Larids use Caribou Island as a staging point in fall, and a **Least Tern** was a welcome surprise to one visiting birder in mid July. The highest number of gulls is in September when there are usually small numbers of **Ringbilled and Bonaparte's Gulls** and an occasional **Blackheaded Gull or Caspian Tern**. The latter are, however, much more likely in late July when they are driven from their preferred Prince Edward Island beaches. Shorebirds are varied, although only **Semipalmated Plover and Semipalmated Sandpiper** with totals of **200+** could be considered numerous. **Piping Plover, Killdeer, Whimbrel and Red Knot** are outnumbered by **Ruddy Turnstone, Lesser Yellowlegs, Shortbilled Dowitcher and Least Sandpiper**. **Pectoral and Whiterumped Sandpipers** are seen among the later arrivals when **Purple Sandpiper and Rednecked Phalarope** are likely.

Pictou itself is best known for its nesting colony of **130+ pairs of Doublecrested Cormorant** on the old pilings just east of Highway 106 at Abercrombie. The first birds arrive back in April and young may still be visible in the nests well into fall. My highest count is **1900** in September, but a more normal count would be **400**. The difference cannot be entirely blamed on a pair of **Great Horned Owl** which feed young cormorants to their nestlings in June!

Very few visits have been made in spring, but **9 Barrow's Goldeneye** in mid April and summering **Sora and Black Tern** indicate the possibilities. The mixture of farmland, forest and marsh offers boreal and southern species. **Cliff and Bank Swallows** have established several colonies, and there have been several sightings of **Purple Martin**. In spring and late summer, **Eastern Bluebird and Warbling Vireo** rate as more unusual migrants, while an early October flock of **100 Horned Lark** and a high count of **46 Bohemian Waxwing** are both very high for the region.

Some of the more notable fall migrants have included **Yellowcrowned Night Heron and American Coot**, and there have been a few **Northern Gannet, Leach's Stormpetrel and Black Guillemot** inshore in October, but the season really belongs to the diving ducks. **Common Eider, Whitewinged and Black Scoters** pass by in good numbers before the first of the **400+ Greater Scaup, 300** wintering **Common** and somewhat less common **Redbreasted Mergansers** appear. **Common and Barrow's Goldeneyes** join them, and an occasional **Canvasback or King Eider** might be seen. The only other common visitors in fall are **150+ Bonaparte's Gull** in October — a few **Blackheaded Gull** among them now winter.

One last area close to Pictou can also be reached by driving east on Highway 104 from Truro to Stellarton and taking a minor road south from the Heather turnoff. This is Hopewell where Harry and Calvin Brennan have made a habit of finding the nests of birds of prey or providing well-used nest boxes. They can always locate resident pairs of **Northern Goshawk, Broadwinged and Redtailed Hawks, Great Horned and Saw-whet Owls**. **Osprey and Bald Eagle** nest in the area and are not hard to find, but Harry has also tracked down **Sharpshinned and Cooper's Hawks, American Kestrel, Barred, Boreal and Longeared Owls**. Seeing a family of **Saw-whet Owls** in their chocolate attire or being buzzed by an angry **Barred Owl** are experiences not to be missed. **Spruce Grouse** are quite common in the boreal forests of the Pictou highlands, **Pileated Woodpecker** is quite widespread and both **Yellowbellied Sapsucker and Blackbacked Woodpecker** far from unusual. Harry also had a male **Rubythroated Hummingbird** coming to his feeder on my June visit.

Hopewell Marsh, stretching for more than a mile along the railway tracks, consists of cattails, reeds, rushes and small bushes occupied by a resident population of muskrats. This is a great location for breeding **American Bittern and Sora**, with a few **Black and Ringnecked Ducks, Common Merganser, and Virginia Rail** flown in for good measure. **Killdeer and Mourning Dove** also nest, and there have been fall records of **Yellowcrowned Night Heron and American Coot**. The most common birds are, however, not waterbirds at all, but **75+ pairs of Cliff Swallow**. **Chestnutsided, Blackburnian and Blackthroated Blue Warblers** reach their regular notheasterly limits here, and **Chimney Swift** are frequent sights overhead in summer. A trip to the local blueberry barrens could add a few passerines in fall, and the seepage fens attract **Rubycrowned Kinglet, Palm and Tennessee Warblers, and Lincoln's Sparrow** to the bordering heaths.

The Trafalgar area is undergoing a transformation with the road from Stellarton being upgraded as a major highway into the Liscombe Sanctuary. I made an early morning visit in mid June and turned up **Spruce Grouse, Great Horned Owl, American Woodcock, Yellowbellied Flycatcher, Palm, Blackpoll and Canada Warblers, and Lincoln's Sparrows** before highway construction drowned out the songs.

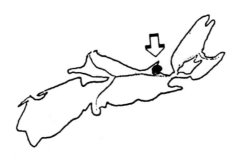

ANTIGONISH AREA

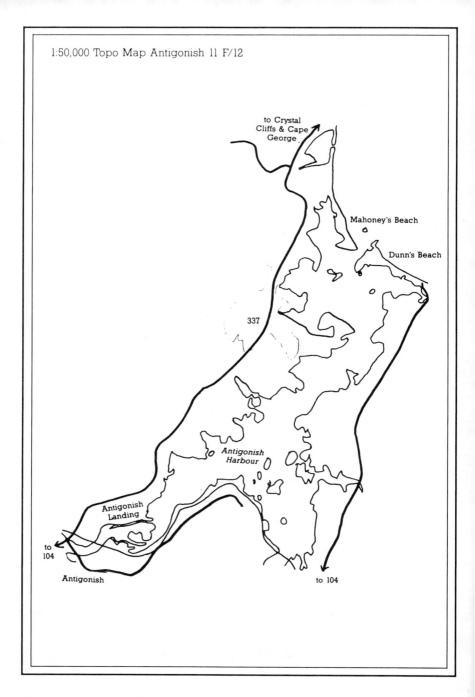

1:50,000 Topo Map Antigonish 11 F/12

to Crystal
Cliffs & Cape
George

Mahoney's Beach

Dunn's Beach

337

Antigonish
Harbour

Antigonish
Landing

to
104

Antigonish

to 104

Antigonish comes from a Micmac name that translates as "where branches were broken off trees by bears gathering beechnuts". The bears, beeches and Micmacs are in short supply now, but the name has been retained by the residents whose Gaelic upbringing is reflected in farming and the Highland Games. Roland Chiasson and Stephen Flemming have really put Antigonish on the birding map, although good birding sites are few and far between. The best are found from Cape George to Cape Jack north and east of Antigonish.

Cape George is reached by taking Highway 245 north through Malignant Cove or the Sunrise Trail — Highway 337. The headland is a good place to look for pelagics, although few people have ventured here in summer. Rather more people seek out Crystal Cliffs where colonies of **Great Cormorant and Black Guillemot** share the limelight with feeding **Bald Eagle and Osprey**. Permission to visit the area should be obtained from Saint FX University in Antigonish who help maintain a watch. Groups of **Bonaparte's Gull** pause here in spring and fall, and a small number of **Canada Geese** winter.

Dunn's and Mahoney's Beaches lie on opposite sides of the harbour. Both beaches have nesting **Piping Plover** and these have received special protection in the way of a vehicle ban. The white beach, dunes and grassland areas are flanked by tidal flats which have good numbers of migrant waterfowl and shorebirds. There is also an island **Common and Arctic Tern** colony which may draw an occasional **Black or Roseate Tern**, and a good number of **Great Blackbacked Gulls** year round. Large groups of ducks are common around the harbour mouth, where the regular wintering species are joined by **Lesser Scaup. Great Blue Heron** is a very common visitor to the flats where **Semipalmated Plover, Least and Semipalmated Sandpipers** are plentiful. **Lesser Golden Plover, Whimbrel, Willet, Hudsonian Godwit and Pectoral Sandpiper** all feed here in fall.

Black Guillemot

The best birding is undoubtedly at the Antigonish Landing Wildlife Management Area which was given to the province as a sanctuary for waterfowl and birds of prey. The 500 acres of fresh and saltwater marshes lie next to the estuary mudflats, and there are some conifer stands. Permission is needed to walk the marshes, but access by road is not restricted. The only restriction is in winter when the road may not be ploughed, but few birds are likely at this time. In spring the estuary hosts a number of **Mallard, Northern Pintail, Greater Scaup, Bufflehead, Common and Barrow's Goldeneyes, and Hooded Merganser** as early as April. Other spring visitors have included **Common Loon, Piedbilled Grebe, Canada Goose and Gadwall**. The locally-nesting **American Wigeon and Ringnecked Duck** wait until May. Several other ducks nest, with **Black Duck** common and **Greenwinged and Bluewinged Teal, and Wood Duck** in small numbers.

Not that waterfowl are the only attraction — far from it. At least **3 Bald Eagle and 8 Osprey** nest in the area, and there is also a chance that a few pairs of **Greater Yellowlegs** may breed. **Northern Harrier and Great Horned Owl** have also appeared in spring and could nest. **Killdeer and Willet** both breed in adjoining areas, and there are often **Bonaparte's Gull and Black Tern** in August when the shorebird migration is well underway. A male **Eastern Bluebird** in early July was unfortunately a stray.

Fall is the best time to look for shorebirds, which are somewhat inhibited by the high water levels maintained for nesting ducks. **Semipalmated Sandpiper** are very common and may stay into November, but there are also fair numbers of **Semipalmated Plover, Killdeer and Lesser Yellowlegs**. Both **Willet and Solitary Sandpiper** pass through in August and early September, and there has been a possible **Western Sandpiper**. More visits would probably reveal more rarities. When the nesting ducks have left, Antigonish Landing has good numbers of migrants. **Ruddy Duck, Redhead and Hooded Merganser** are all quite regular in October, and all commoner species are well represented, including **Mallard**.

Nearby Pomquet also has **Piping Plover** nesting along its sand beach, and this is another good place to look for **Osprey** — as many as **9 pairs** nest in the area and can be seen fishing by the Pomquet River mouth. There is also a colony of **Great Cormorant and Black Guillemot** at Monk's Head, and nesting **Willet and Common Tern** on the marshes. **Lesser Yellowlegs** are common on fall migration, when a few **Piping Plover and Sanderling** run the sand beach. The same kind of variety is likely at Monastery where there is a sandbar, but I have not seen any reports recently.

Other places to visit from this site

An alternative route to Cape George is along the Sunrise Trail east of New Glasgow. The large island guarding Merigomish Harbour is variously known as Big, or Merigomish, Island. The turnoff to the island, which is really a peninsula, is just beyond Lower Barney's River Bridge at Exit 27A. Although storm tides may occasionally cut off access, you can usually drive west from here beside grassland, marshes and flats and a public beach to a harbour inlet. Ducks and geese rest in the shallow waters to the south. **Black Duck** are the commonest species, but other dabbling ducks, mergansers and a few other diving ducks regularly join them.

Visitors in summer should watch out for the soft shoulders which are every bit as annoying as the poison ivy in the dunes and the swarms of blackfly, mosquito, horsefly and deerfly on the beaches. A ridge of dunes protects the bar, and the road is built on an improvised seawall flanked by pastures and fields on one side and fresh and saltwater on the others. The typical breeding songbird (for want of a better word!) is the **Sharptailed Sparrow** which competes with the **Savannah Sparrow** for chart status, but **Rubythroated Hummingbird, Yellowbellied Sapsucker, Alder and Least Flycatchers, Gray Jay, Boreal Chickadee, Brown Creeper, Winter Wren, Gray Catbird, Northern Parula, Magnolia, Blackthroated Blue and Mourning Warblers, Bobolink, Rusty Blackbird, Pine Siskin, Red and Whitewinged Crossbills** were all noted by Gerry Bennett in and around what is now called Melnerby Beach Park adjacent to Big Island.

American Bittern, Greenwinged and Bluewinged Teal, Sora and American Woodcock can all be found in summer, and **Northern Goshawk, Sharpshinned Hawk, Osprey, Barred and Saw-whet Owls** are frequently seen in the area. Most of the nesting terns are **Arctic Tern**, but an occasional **Black or Caspian Tern** can be expected after mid July. A few **Piping Plover and Willet** may breed, but most shorebirds are migrants. **Shortbilled Dowitcher** numbers are quite high in late summer, when **Whimbrel, Ruddy Turnstone and Red Knot** are equally conspicuous among the early **Least, Whiterumped and Semipalmated Sandpipers. Common Snipe and Lesser Yellowlegs** are both found in good numbers in September when a stray **Rednecked Phalarope** may be blown in. An occasional **Blackbilled Cuckoo, Common Nighthawk or Chimney Swift** may chance by in late summer.

Other pelagic species, such as **Leach's Storm-petrel and Black Guillemot**, are more likely to be seen in October, but late August-early September **Least Tern and Glossy Ibis** added a brief touch of the tropics. **Northern Shoveler** are also regular in fall, but **Common and Redthroated Loons, Horned Grebe, Whitewinged and Surf Scoters** are far more common from October into the winter. **Great Blue Heron** also feed here at low tide and roost in the dunes. **Northern Harrier and Roughlegged Hawk** are frequent October visitors. Fall flocks of **Water Pipit and Lapland Longspur** are as large as anywhere in the province.

I am including a number of sites on the Atlantic coast in Guysboro County mainly because there is no major birding site. The first is Tobacco Island which is located at the entrance to Gegogan Bay east of Liscomb. Like other islands of the Eastern Shore Island Management Area, it has several colonies of seabirds. About **400 pairs of Common Eider and 200 pairs of Doublecrested Cormorant** share the island with **Great Blue Heron and Leach's Storm-petrel** colonies. **Blackpoll Warbler and Fox Sparrow** are the most interesting songbirds in summer, but there have been some very interesting visitors from late April to late October. Spring can be very productive with **Rednecked Grebe, Canada Goose, Black Duck, Northern Pintail, Osprey, Merlin, Willet and Purple Sandpiper** in water and shore locations, and **Olivesided Flycatcher, Gray Catbird and Bobolink** in the woods and grassland. **Rubythroated Hummingbird** has also been seen on the island, and a few more visits could add to a late August **Yellowheaded Blackbird**. Shorebirds are the most frequent fall visitors, but storms can blow in a **Northern Gannet or Red Phalarope**.

A little further on east of Sherbrook is Wine Harbour, which can be reached by taking a turn off Marine Drive — Highway 7. **Great Blue Heron** nest most years and there have been a few nonbreeding **Black Tern** in mid July. The small settlements have several colonies of **Cliff Swallow**, and boreal birds are often driven out of the spruce-fir forests by bad weather. **Spruce Grouse** are widespread in Guysboro County, and **Blackbacked Woodpecker** is fairly regularly seen. The sheltered waters are also popular with **200 +**

Doublecrested Cormorant from mid April to October when most of the ducks, especially **Common Eider**, peak — **Bufflehead** may sometimes summer in small numbers. The most interesting shorebirds are nesting **Killdeer and American Woodcock**, and this is not an area to look for large numbers. **Yellowbilled and Blackbilled Cuckoos** are fairly regular in October, and there have been midsummer records of **Roughwinged Swallow and Philadelphia Vireo**.

The Canso area juts out into the Atlantic Ocean off Highway 316, and this partially explains the number of interesting birds found here — the lack of local birders probably explains why there are not more. A late October hurricane deposited small numbers of **Snowy Egret, Black Skimmer and Forster's Tern** in 1968, but it has only been the last five years that other unusual vagrants have been found. **Great and Snowy Egrets** are probably regular in spring, but a **Redshouldered Hawk** in mid May, **Black Tern** in mid June and **Blue Grosbeak** in mid-late May were probably just transients. Fall has a better selection of birds. **Common Terns** may linger into October, which is the best time to look for **Common Murre and Caspian Tern. Great Horned and Short-eared Owls** may nest near Canso, but other migrants such as **Longeared, Snowy and Boreal Owls** certainly don't.

The best site may well be Hazel Hill which has recently been "discovered" by local birders. **Merlin and Blackbacked Woodpecker** may nest in the area, and **Northern Parula** are very common in June, but the main attraction has been a number of notable strays. **Redheaded Woodpecker, Scissortailed Flycatcher, Bluegray Gnatcatcher and Yellowheaded Blackbird** have so far been seen in fall and early winter, and **2 Little Blue Heron** have appeared in mid August. In the spring of 1988, Nancy Peters had a "flood" of **Indigo Buntings, Blue and Rosebreasted Grosbeaks.** The birds stayed only a day or so, long enough to replenish themselves after a harrowing flight. Undoubtedly, more surprises await anyone intrepid enough to spend some time here.

The last area on the Marine Drive is Guysboro which lies at the head of Chedabucto Bay. The coastal highway from Canso offers a chance of seeing **hundreds of Leach's Storm-petrel** inshore in mid June, and rafts of **Whitewinged, Black and Surf Scoters** in May and October. Much greater numbers of pelagics are almost certainly found a little further out — as the tragic oil spill all too vividly demonstrated a few years ago. Boreal species are common in the wooded areas around Guysboro , with **Olivesided Flycatcher, Boreal Chickadee and Pine Grosbeak** very conspicuous. **Cedar Waxwing and American Goldfinch** are also common, and there may have been some broods of **Least Sandpiper** raised along the coast. Mid fall **Dickcissels** are quite normal, and both **American Coot and Yellow Rail** indicate that marshes and wetter fields might be worth checking out in fall. A recent early December visit to the Canso Causeway revealed as many as **500 Bonaparte's and 7 Blackheaded Gulls**. This impressive collection of small gulls attracted an immature **Ross's Gull**. A second bird recently appeared in mid June.

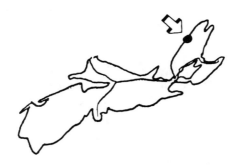

CHETICAMP AREA

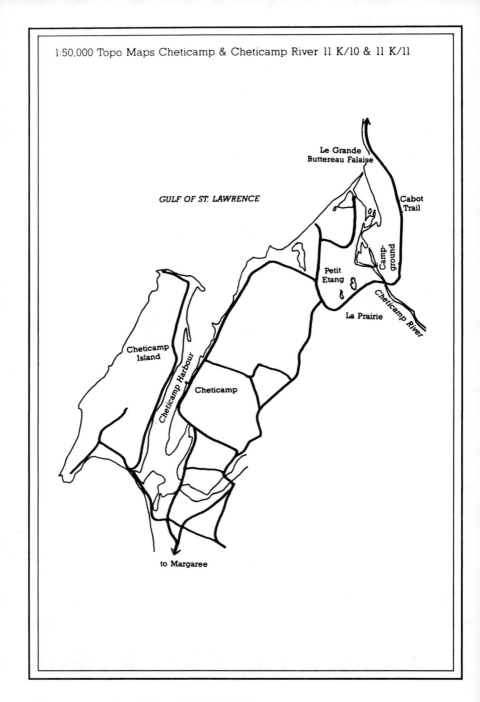

1:50,000 Topo Maps Cheticamp & Cheticamp River 11 K/10 & 11 K/11

GULF OF ST. LAWRENCE

Le Grande
Buttereau Falaise

Cabot
Trail

Camp-
ground

Petit
Etang

Cheticamp River

La Prairie

Cheticamp
Island

Cheticamp Harbour

Cheticamp

to Margaree

The Cape Breton Highlands area is one of the most scenic anywhere in the province, which explains the popularity of the Cabot Trail which runs through it from Baddeck. Most of the area is within the boundaries of Cape Breton Highlands National Park which straddles both coastlines. This is an area of wild, windswept cliffs and mountains, bogs, barrens, rushing rivers and wooded canyons. It is also an excellent place to study birds—as I did when I undertook the first year of the park's avifaunal study in 1977. One of the best features of the park is that almost every site is accessible by the extensive trail system.

The best way to enjoy the park is to drive from west to east, from Cheticamp to Ingonish. There is a good reason for this—fog is a constant problem in the mountains, but if it is clear at Cheticamp there's an excellent chance it's clear all through. Ingonish is more likely to be clear and is not such a good indicator of weather conditions in the mountains. Cheticamp is located in the heart of the Acadian section of Inverness County and there are a number of indications of this in the community. The large campground just inside the park boundary is an excellent place to stay, but it does get crowded on weekends.

The first recommended site is actually just outside the park. Connected to the mainland by a sandbar which provides the base for the road, Cheticamp Island is a good place to start. A dirt road leads right from the main road to the lighthouse where there are nesting **Great Cormorant, Black Guillemot and Blacklegged Kittiwake** on the cliffs. Pelagics may come close to the headland, although porpoises, dolphins and whales are more likely. Both **Great Blue Heron and Northern Harrier** are increasing and may well nest somewhere on the island. The saltmarshes and beaches by the road are good for ducks, including **Mallard and American Wigeon**, and for stray herons and egrets, especially **Little Blue Heron**.

Shorebirds are very much a fall feature, with enough **Lesser Golden Plover** on the fields to make **Buffbreasted Sandpiper** very likely in late August-early October. Most species can be seen, but numbers are very low from late July to early October and the only rarity I have heard of is a **Baird's Sandpiper** in early September. Gulls and terns are more common on the water and along the beaches, and I have seen **Blackheaded Gull and Caspian Tern** in the peak counts at the end of August. The channel between the island and the mainland is favoured by **Whitewinged and Surf Scoters** late in the fall, and **Dovekie** and other alcids are common around the island in early winter.

I have been cod-jigging from Cheticamp, and I heartily recommend it if the wind is down and you have company to cook for. Saltmarshes form a major component of the surrounding area, so nesting ducks and marshbirds are widespread. **American Bittern and Great Blue Heron** can be seen almost anywhere, but Petit Etang is probably the best place to look for **Piedbilled Grebe, Little Blue Heron and Snowy Egret**, all of which appear frequently. The small fresh and saltwater swamps at La Prairie have had these species, plus occasional **Black Tern** and regular visits from **Longeared and Shorteared Owls** in early fall. **Common Nighthawk** nest in good numbers and can be seen at dusk and dawn.

Shorebirds make good use of the muddy harbour fringes at low tide — **Pectoral Sandpipers** have even picked up the habit of cleaning up after fishermen by the landing stages! Flocks of **Semipalmated Plover** may contain a much paler **Piping Plover**, and there are always a few **Greater and Lesser Yellowlegs, Least, Whiterumped or Semipalmated Sandpipers** with them. The coastal marshes attract other species, including a mid June **Ruff**, and the headlands have a few **Whimbrel** in late summer. Gulls are very conspicuous harbour residents from late July, when there are a few **Ringbilled Gull**, to October, which is the best time to look for **Blackheaded Gull** among the **Common and Arctic Terns, and Bonaparte's Gulls** feeding in the harbour. The regularly wintering **Iceland Gulls** are joined by a few **Blacklegged Kittiwake** in early winter.

Dabbling ducks may be seen on the marshes from late April to early October, and a few pairs breed. But this is Acadian country and ducks are part of the menu year-round, so very few birds stay long. The later flocks in fall may contain a **Mallard** or two and perhaps a **Bufflehead**. Songbirds are quite well represented with **Fox Sparrow** nesting close to the Cheticamp River where flocks of wintering sparrows could be expected to contain lingering and rare species. A few **Redbreasted Nuthatch** also nest in the conifers, and there have been some nesting **Rubythroated Hummingbird and Loggerhead Shrike** — the latter a very rare bird at any time of year now.

The Cheticamp River floodplain is accessible at several points from the campground and offers a wide variety of breeding species and some unusual migrants. There are pools for waterfowl, including **Mallard and Bluewinged Teal**, wet areas for **Great Blue Heron** and the occasional southern stray, and marshes by the rivermouth for shorebirds. Numbers are never large, but there is good variety. Insects also swarm along the river, which is why hirundines and flycatchers are so common. **Barn Swallow** nests can be found in the picnic shelters and other buildings, **Cliff Swallow** can be seen throughout the summer, and you can look for a few **Purple Martin** in May. **Eastern Kingbird** perch along the river, while wood edges and glades are favoured by **Alder Flycatcher and Eastern Wood-pewee**.

This is also a good place to study warblers. **Tennessee Warbler and Northern Waterthrush** are typical of the scrubby growth alongside the campground, and **Mourning Warbler** becomes commoner as you approach the Salmon Falls trail. Most of the breeding warblers are found in the tentsite section of the campground which is highly recommended to birders. **Solitary Vireo, Northern Parula and American Redstart** are common in these mixed woods, while **Yellow Warbler and Common Yellowthroat** are found by the river. A few **Winter Wren** have returned to the swampier woods after recovering from a population decline in the 1970s, and **Cedar Waxwing** parties in late summer suggest they may nest here. **Rosebreasted Grosbeak** certainly breeds, and there are often family groups of **Evening Grosbeak and Purple Finch**, too.

The Salmon Pools trail starts from the edge of the trailer section of the campground and leads upstream to a series of pools popular with fishermen, hikers and families. The riverine woods are varied, although there are few conifers. Most hardwoods grow in pure stands — with yellow and white birch, sugar maple and beech both widespread and of large size. The habitat variety makes this steepsided canyon one of the best birding trails in the park with over 70 species found within two miles of the campground.

Northern Goshawk and Bald Eagle fly over the trail, and both **Broadwinged Hawk and Barred Owl** can occur during the summer months. The rock and gravel banks support many pairs of **Spotted Sandpiper** whose young can be seen scampering along the trail in July. Flycatchers and woodpeckers are common, with **Least Flycatcher** widespread and the chance of hearing **Great Crested Flycatcher** in the hardwood stands. Vireos and warblers are also well-represented, with **Redeyed Vireo and Oven-**

bird abundant all along the trail and **Solitary Vireo and Blackburnian Warbler** at some stops. Migrants in late August are worth checking out as **Philadelphia Vireo** is often seen by the river and rarer species are likely. Both **Rosebreasted Grosbeak and Purple Finch** are common in summer when a flash of red might betray the presence of a **Scarlet Tanager**. Boreal species are not a feature of the trail, although the higher section has **Yellowrumped and Blackthroated Warblers** in good numbers, but there may be a few **Pine Grosbeak** along the way.

Baybreasted Warbler

The other two trails in this area offer a variety of warblers. The short Lake trail turns to the left off the Salmon Falls trail just after climbing from the campground. This is an excellent place to watch **Cape May, Blackburnian, Blackpoll and Baybreasted Warblers** in early August, and sparrows are common in the shorter growth. A better trail in terms of variety is the Acadian trail which has a fairly long initial climb from the campground and a return along the Robert Brook valley. If you don't have much time to spend, a spur trail takes you back to the Visitor Centre. The trail passes through a number of very different habitats, especially in the steep lower section. You pass from mixed woods to overmature spruce and then skirt open parkland to a combination of mixed woods, open spruce and hardwoods higher up. There are even rock barrens on the summit.

The lower sections provide the greatest variety, but a climb to the top may be rewarded by **Northern Harrier and Spruce Grouse** in summer and migrating raptors in fall. **Blackbacked Woodpecker** is possible here among the commoner species, and there are a few flycatchers, but the warblers form the most significant part of the songbird population. Most species are commoner here than anywhere else around Cheticamp — **Cape May, Blackpoll and Baybreasted Warblers** are particularly abundant in the spruces. There are also a few **Solitary Vireo and Mourning Warbler** and harder-to-find **Brown Creeper, Redbreasted Nuthatch, Graycheeked Thrush and Blackburnian Warbler**. Late in August, the spur trail is very productive with flocks of **Pine Siskin and American Goldfinch** close to the trailhead. A little further up the slope, migrant warblers may include **Cape May and Nashville Warblers, and Northern Waterthrush**. The whole trail takes about four hours to complete, while a walk up to the plateau and back takes a little over two hours with stops along the way.

The last trail in the Cheticamp area makes use of an old road to an abandoned Acadian settlement. The trail starts in the shadow of the red cliff face of Grande Falaise (Big Cliff) — best seen at sunset when it glows like a lantern, and leads to a bluff overlooking the mouth of the Cheticamp River. This high meadow is perhaps unique on this coast and has a number of breeding sparrows, including **Lincoln's Sparrow**. The trail, which has a self-guiding pamphlet, leads through alders, secondgrowth and mature spruce to the wet meadow and always has a good selection of nesting species.

The small coastal marsh at the start of the trail has had as many as **20 Spotted Sandpiper** feeding among the seaweed-covered rocks in early August. You should also look up to see **Bald Eagle and Redtailed Hawk** riding the thermals of Grand Falaise. **Merlin** are more likely to be seen along the trail in September when flocks of warblers and sparrows provide a steady supply of food. The steep slopes covered with secondgrowth and alder often have several warblers, but the best habitat is among the mature spruces where **Magnolia and Yellowrumped Warblers** are common, and **Blackburnian and Baybreasted Warblers** present in small numbers. The dawn and dusk chorus also includes a number of thrushes, but the quality of melodic interpretation is much lower on the meadow where sparrows are dominant. The barachois at the rivermouth can be studied from here — ducks and shorebirds are quite likely in late summer and early fall. One final word — don't leave your insect repellent in the car because mosquitoes and blackflies can be wicked on this trail!

Other places to visit from this site

The recently-created Ceilidh Trail — Highway 19 — is an alternative access point to the Cheticamp shore. A selection of riverine woods, sandy beaches and rocky points offer good birding opportunities with a stop at Lake Ainslie recommended for waterfowl. You can drive around the lake, but I prefer the gravel road on the west shore as it is not crowded with holidaymakers. Several broods of **Ringnecked Duck** are raised here, and a careful check might reveal a few **Piedbilled Grebe** in late summer. Other ducks are likely, and I suspect **Redhead, Lesser Scaup and Ruddy Duck** could turn up here if their range expansions continue.

The access from Highway 105 is along Highway 395 from Whycocomagh — one of the best places to see **Bald Eagle** at close range by Bras d'Or Lake. These birds are used to passing cars and sit on roadside snags to watch for fish. As long as you don't get out of the car, they are unlikely to fly. **Great Blue Heron, Doublecrested Cormorant and Ringnecked Duck** are also common, and I have watched late summer parties of **50+ Common Nighthawk** streaming by. Later in the fall, rafts of **Black and Surf Scoters** start to appear after the **Common**, and sometimes **Black Terns** have left. **Belted Kingfishers** are less mindful of the cold weather and sometimes overwinter. A similar area a little further along Highway 105 at the Nyanza delta has seven duck species, including **Bluewinged Teal**, and colonies of **Great Blue Heron and Common Tern. Bald Eagle and Osprey** both nest, and the hardwood stands have a few **Pileated Woodpecker**. This would also seem to be a good place to look for **Chimney Swift, Rubythroated Hummingbird, Scarlet Tanager and Rosebreasted Grosbeak**. There are usually a few **Cliff Swallows** with the **Barn Swallow** flocks in summer, and **Alder Flycatcher, Common Grackle and Song Sparrow** are common.

If you take the Nyanza exit from Highway 105, you will cross the divide northwest of Finlayson and see the floodplain of the Margaree River. This supports a wide variety of waterbirds, as well as a good cross-section of nesting flycatchers, thrushes and warblers. Much of the plain is farmland now with a high breeding population of **Barn, Tree and Cliff Swallows, Redwinged Blackbird and Bobolink. Purple Martin** is a strong possibility, too. The variety of woodlands ensures a good variety of nesting warblers and finches, especially **Purple Finch** which is common in late summer. The Northeast Margaree River leads to boreal habitats with a good assortment of woodland birds including **Spruce Grouse**. The Margaree River valley has a few nesting **Bald Eagle, Northern Harrier and American Kestrel**, and the climate is mild enough in winter to have allowed **Greenwinged Teal** to stay year round.

Margaree Harbour offers a fine sand beach and excellent views of the valley. The estuary has large flocks of **Doublecrested Cormorant** in spring and fall — often with a few **Great Cormorant** among them, and the wintering ducks include **Common Goldeneye and Oldsquaw**. Larids and shorebirds are also quite common by the roadbridge. A few **Lesser Golden Plover and Whimbrel** feast on crowberries on the small headland, and there are **Least and Semipalmated Sandpipers** on the sand beaches at low tide. **Greater and Lesser Yellowlegs** also feed here and on the farm fields where they join **Semipalmated and Blackbellied Plovers** early in the fall. **Whiterumped Sandpiper and Dunlin** are frequently seen before wintering **Purple Sandpiper** arrive.

Cap Rouge to the east of Grande Falaise contains a variety of habitats from the shingle and sand beach to steep slopes covered with alder, cherry and shrubs preferred by **Mourning Warbler and Gray Catbird** — here to Corney Brook is the only regular breeding area. The beaches attract few shorebirds early in fall and there are usually more gulls than anything else, but **Great Cormorant and Common Eider** are regularly seen offshore and **Black Guillemot** nests somewhere in the vicinity. Corney Brook is more rewarding with a few **Mourning Warbler and Common Yellowthroat** by the campground and an excellent trail along the river canyon. **Ruffed Grouse** are common near the trailhead and there has been a **Greenbacked Heron** in late summer. **Redeyed Vireo and American Redstart** are the commonest songbirds, but there are also a good number of **Blackburnian Warbler** in the mixed woods. The trail is good for warblers throughout August and into early September.

Once you climb up French Mountain on the Cabot Trail, you are entering true boreal forest for the first time. Especially common are **Yellowrumped and Blackpoll Warblers, Pine Grosbeak and Darkeyed Junco**. The trail around a bog has nesting **Northern Harrier** and regular visits from **Greater Yellowlegs**, but the best birding is along the Fishing Cove Lake and Benjie's Lake trails. These start out in scrub and tuckamoor and end in mature black spruce with fern cover by bog lakes. A few **Osprey, Black Duck and Greenwinged Teal** nest by the ponds, but the main attraction is the variety of boreal songbirds. **Cape May, Baybreasted and Mourning Warblers** are found in small numbers on the Benjie's Lake trail, and **Pine Grosbeak and Fox Sparrow** are both very common on the Fishing Cove Lake trail which starts out along an old road through stunted spruce with a mixture of maple, cherry and mountain ash among white birch and heaths. The berries attract large numbers of warblers, especially **Magnolia, Yellowrumped and Blackpoll Warblers**, and sparrows. A **Redtailed Hawk** can often be found perched on the taller trees in early fall, and **Spruce Grouse** are possible at both locations.

The Fishing Cove trail starts out in an old burn area and then leads through mixed and coniferous woods to end at an attractive open meadow. The lower sections of the trail offer varied habitats close to the stream with **Magnolia and Mourning Warblers** among the commonest breeding warblers. One of the most widespread nesting songbirds appears to be the **Evening Grosbeak** which occurs in family parties all along the trail, and it is worth checking the migrant warblers in late August as I have seen **Orangecrowned Warbler** near the trailhead. Birds of prey are quite often seen on the trail, especially **Sharpshinned Hawk and Northern Harrier** along the coast and **Redtailed Hawk** higher up the mountain. A few **Roughlegged Hawk** are regular between here and Pleasant Bay later in the fall and in early spring.

Pleasant Bay was not accessible by road until 1927, but its location on the Cabot Trail makes it a good place to stop for a meal now. A short road north to Red River might turn up a few **Northern Oriole and American Goldfinch**, and more mature stands support **Rosebreasted Grosbeak and Pine Siskin. Common and Arctic Terns** fish close to shore, and it is not uncommon to find **Caspian Tern** when the **Bonaparte's Gull** parties arrive. Although shorebirds are scarce early on, **Ruddy Turnstone and Dunlin** are regular in late August-early October, and there may be a few **Purple Sandpiper** wintering. **Bald Eagle** is the most likely raptor, although **Roughlegged Hawk** can be seen on migration. Late fall rafts may contain a few **King Eider**.

The steepsided canyons of the Grand Anse valley drain into Pleasant Bay. The rapid drainage favours sugar maple, yellow birch and red oak throughout, and white spruce parkland in wetter sites. **Eastern Wood-pewee, Redeyed Vireo and American Redstart** indicate the hardwood nature of the woods, although the largest summer flocks are of **Pine Siskin and American Goldfinch** — I have counted **200+** of the former in the small picnic area by the Cabot Trail in early August. A careful search reveals a few **Least Flycatcher, Scarlet Tanager and Rosebreasted Grosbeak**, as well as good numbers of **Nashville and Blackburnian Warblers**.

This is also an excellent place to look for birds of prey. **Broadwinged Hawk** is at least as common as **Redtailed Hawk**, and a twilight visit will likely flush out a few **Great Horned Owls**. Other hawks are more of a migration feature, with **Sharpshinned Hawk and Merlin** frequently seen in September. Pleasant Bay often has **Cedar Waxwing and Evening Grosbeak** in late summer when an occasional **Rubythroated Hummingbird** may zip by.

The North Aspy River is the last stop before the Cabot Trail reaches the Cape North coast. A gravel road leads from the warden station at Big Intervale through open spruce parkland to a parking lot by Beulach Ban Falls. You can then walk on a trail through mature maple-birch-beech woods above the river. This is an excellent trail for nesting warblers with as many as 16 species present, and it is also good for flycatchers and thrushes. The parkland by the river flats has several pairs of **Lincoln's Sparrow** and some **Yellowbellied Flycatcher**, but the real interest is just beyond the falls. The number of warblers builds as you climb up the mountain slopes — **Northern Parula and Blackburnian Warbler** are particularly noticeable, although the songs of **Ovenbird and American Redstart** dominate the summer chorus. There are also a few **Rosebreasted Grosbeak** and good numbers of **Pine Siskin**, and the twilight is a good time to listen for **Veery** in the mixed woods and **Gray Catbird** close to the start of the gravel road. A few pairs of **Belted Kingfisher and Pileated Woodpecker** also nest along the North Aspy.

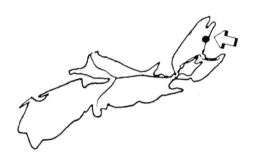

INGONISH AREA

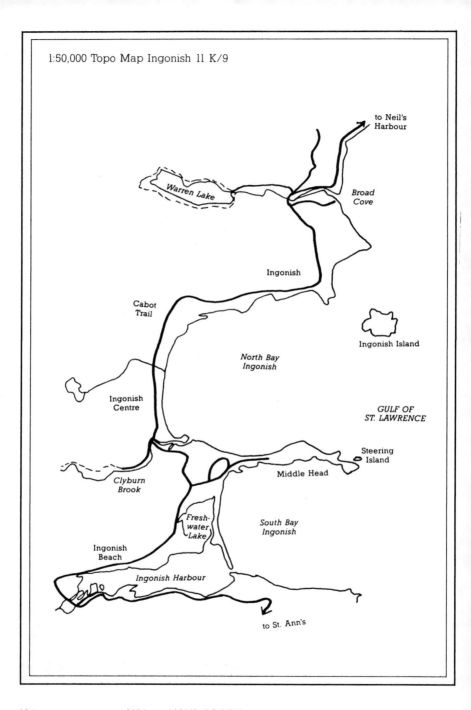

1:50,000 Topo Map Ingonish 11 K/9

to Neil's Harbour

Warren Lake

Broad Cove

Ingonish

Cabot Trail

Ingonish Island

North Bay Ingonish

Ingonish Centre

GULF OF ST. LAWRENCE

Steering Island

Middle Head

Clyburn Brook

Fresh-water Lake

South Bay Ingonish

Ingonish Beach

Ingonish Harbour

to St. Ann's

The east coast of Cape Breton Highlands National Park is less mountainous than the west coast with a somewhat drier climate in summer. These facts are reflected in the forest cover which is not as rich and has rather more conifers at lower altitudes. The northern section is a continuation of the boreal forests of Cape North, but the coastal strip around Ingonish is more reminiscent of habitats to the south. I have undertaken the Cape North breeding bird survey route several times and it underlines the forest diversity. Starting at Capstick near the northernmost cape in Nova Scotia and ending at Neil's Harbour, this route regularly produces over 70 species which is extremely high for the Maritimes.

The best birding in the park is from Broad Cove to Ingonish Harbour. This has everything a birder could ask for — many different habitats, easy access and lots of birds. You can camp at Broad Cove or below Cape Smokey and walk the many trails any time from early May to late September without the risk of disappointment. You might not see everything you came for, but you will see a good selection of waterfowl, birds of prey, gamebirds, woodpeckers and songbirds.

Broad Cove campground consists mainly of open parkland with aspens and birches, or mixed woods, both on sandy soils. The beach is smaller than others in the park so the campsites are rarely filled to capacity. **Osprey and Bald Eagle** often roost by the pond at the mouth of Warren Brook and can be seen fishing in the morning and evening. **Common Loon and Great Cormorant** are regular just offshore, and **Black Guillemot** nests are hidden in crevices high in the steep cliff overlooking the beach. The campground has good numbers of spring migrants, including **Baybreasted Warbler and Whitecrowned Sparrow**, and even more songbirds in fall when the budworm moths are a ready source of food for up to 15 species of warblers.

An even better spot can be reached by driving just over a mile on the other side of the Cabot Trail to Warren Lake. The trail loops around the lake and never strays far from the shore. The waters can be quite choppy, but there is usually a **Common Loon** and a few gulls. Most of the trail is in mixed woods — with white spruce, balsam fir, red maple, white birch and sugar maple evident in new growth on my visits ten years ago. There is a spruce stand near the start of the trail and a marshy area at the western end of the lake offering slightly different species. The sandy beach rarely has many shorebirds, but I did find a **Western Sandpiper** here in mid August.

Both **Pileated and Blackbacked Woodpeckers** have nested along the north side of the lake, which is the best place to see **Northern Parula, Baybreasted and Blackburnian Warblers**. **Alder Flycatcher and Common Yellowthroat** are found in the wetter woods at the northwestern corner, where there is sometimes a **Belted Kingfisher**. There are also a few **Rosebreasted and Pine Grosbeaks** raised each summer along the trail which takes about three hours to complete at a leisurely pace. Even when the beach is crowded there are rarely many people on the trail.

The plateau portion of the park can be reached by taking the road to Branch Pond and then walking along the trail. This was the first provincial nesting site of the **Greater Yellowlegs** in the 1940s, and there are still many pairs here although there are now breeding records elsewhere. I would not recommend driving the road unless you have limited time and need to add boreal species to your list—I tried to avoid one of the many potholes and ended up in a ditch one year! The better way is to walk the whole length but this does require a whole day. The first part of the road is often productive enough to make a longer trip unnecessary.

The woods alongside the first part of the trail are mainly mixed woods with a strong softwood bias, including boggy areas with heaths, tamarack and black spruce. This supports families of **Ruffed and Spruce Grouse**—the latter being a little easier to find when the former are on a downswing in their cycle. The small ponds and marshy areas can be counted on for **Common Snipe** and a few **Solitary Sandpiper** from early August. As you walk along the road you can see tall white pine standing above the rest of the forest—these are reminders of the former cover before logging took over. **Mourning Warbler and Evening Grosbeak** are among the commoner species, and there are parties of **Red and Whitewinged Crossbills, Purple Finch and Pine Siskin** feeding in the woods.

From Branch Pond on, the trees become shorter and bogs and barrens take over. **Cedar Waxwing, Cape May Warbler and Purple Finch** nest in the stunted spruce, and there may be a **Northern Goshawk or Merlin** flying over. Once the tree cover ends, the typical birds are **Spruce Grouse, Common Raven, Common Yellowthroat, Pine Grosbeak and Lincoln's Sparrow** in the heaths, and **Greenwinged Teal, Northern Harrier, Greater Yellowlegs and Common Snipe** on the open bogs and ponds. If you walk onto the Lake of Islands plateau you could probably add **Canada Goose**, and I have heard tell of **Willow Ptarmigan** although they haven't been confirmed.

The coastal woods and fields between Ingonish and Ingonish Centre offer a similar selection of birds to habitats inside the park. Spring is a good time to look for flycatchers, including **Eastern Phoebe**, and sometimes southern species such as **Yellowbilled Cuckoo, Rubythroated Hummingbird, Gray Catbird and Dickcissel**. The fall is dominated by ducks and shorebirds which can be seen along the beaches and inshore. Some **Harlequin and Barrow's Goldeneye** winter with the **Whitewinged, Surf and Black Scoters, Common Eider, Greater Scaup, Common Goldeneye and Oldsquaw** flocks in North Bay.

The most interesting birding is in the valley of Clyburn Brook which crosses the golf course just south of Ingonish Centre. The watershed takes in some of the highest land in the park (and the province), and the mixed woods and mature hardwoods constitute a very important habitat for rarer nesting species. While not unique, there is enough variety here to attract **Pileated Woodpecker, Eastern Phoebe, Whitebreasted**

Nuthatch, Philadelphia Vireo, Nashville Warbler and **Scarlet Tanager** each summer. A majority of the flycatchers found in Nova Scotia occur here and there are also large numbers of finches, especially **Pine Siskin**, in the open parkland. **Redeyed Vireo, Ovenbird, Mourning Warbler** and **American Redstart** are all extremely common, and the robin-like song of the **Rosebreasted Grosbeak** is heard in the dawn chorus. A few pairs of **Common Merganser** pursue the trout in the brook, and there may be **Peregrine** on Mount Franie to complement the **Barred Owls** below.

The golf course is an excellent place to look for warblers in late summer, especially **Baybreasted and Blackpoll Warblers**. The golf course also has a few **Dickcissel and Whitecrowned Sparrow** once the links are less active in September. **American Bittern** can be found in the saltmarsh by hole #5, where a **Sora** could also be heard, and a few ducks and **Greater Yellowlegs** often hang out there. **Greenbacked Heron** has turned up in mid June, and **Little Blue Heron, Killdeer and Solitary Sandpiper** have all appeared in late summer.

The 2 mile-long Middle Head trail leads through conifers and more open woods to the windy point which has a small tern colony on Steering Island — there is some debate about whether this name came about because it is a landmark to mariners or because of the tern colony since "stearin" is the local name. Whatever the origin, **Arctic Terns** form the majority of the **70-nest** mixed colony, which sometimes offers temporary shelter to a **Blacklegged Kittiwake or Blackheaded Gull**. A few pairs of **Black Guillemot** nest in the area and **Great Cormorants** are often seen flying by. The point can be rewarding in winter when **Oldsquaw, Common Goldeneye and Dovekie** appear in good numbers and **Harlequin and Barrow's Goldeneye** are infrequent companions.

The softwood section of the trail has most of the park's boreal species, especially **Boreal Chickadee, Hermit Thrush, Red and Whitewinged Crossbills** in summer. Boreal finches are also very common after most other birds have left, and **Red and Whitewinged Crossbills, and Common Redpoll** are numerous on occasions. There have also been winter visits from **Redbreasted Nuthatch, Bohemian Waxwing and Northern Shrike.** I haven't seen any birds of prey at Middle Head, but it would appear to be a good landmark for migrating hawks in both spring and fall.

Boreal Chickadee

The Ingonish Beach area has a greater number of migrants than anywhere else on this coast. This is partly because Freshwater Lake and its surrounding marshes offer a habitat not found elsewhere. Ducks gather here in fall and have included **Lesser Scaup** and even a **Canvasback** in early December. There have also been several visits by **Little Blue Heron and American Coot**. The sandy beach which extends south as a spit across the mouth of Ingonish Harbour is very popular with shorebirds in early fall. **Semipalmated Plover and Ruddy Turnstone** are sometimes fairly common, but the numbers are generally small and no rarities have been reported so far. Few birders tend to bother with this area in summer.

The surrounding woods have a large number of migrants in spring and fall. **Gray Catbird and Blackthroated Blue Warbler** have turned up in spring and early summer, and a careful check of the shrubbery is in order. This is even more true in fall when numbers are higher — a visiting birder added both **Western Kingbird and Say's Phoebe** to the park list early one September. South Bay attracts large numbers of **Oldsquaw, Common Eider and Dovekie** in winter, when a few **Redthroated Loon and Harlequin** may also be seen. Pelagics are possible any time from late summer to early winter, and overwintering passerines are another possibility anywhere in this area — **Yellowheaded Blackbird** being the most notable example. **Threetoed Woodpecker** occasionally leave the conifers after heavy snowfalls, and early spring arrivals like a mid April **Eastern Phoebe** may regret their haste. A word of caution to motorists — Cape Smokey can be treacherous in winter when any combination of ice, sleet, snow and fog can occur.

The campground woods and shrubbery alongside Ingonish Harbour provide rich habitats for breeding songbirds and migrants. This is one of the better places to look for warblers, blackbirds and finches in the summer, and the campground is rarely crowded because it is so far from the bathing beaches. The best time to visit is in early fall when small numbers of ducks, including a good number of **Bluewinged Teal**, and shorebirds, including **Lesser Yellowlegs and Solitary Sandpiper,** linger on their way south. Hawks can be looked for in times of peak migration — I have seen several **Sharpshinned Hawk, Merlin and American Kestrel** in pursuit of small birds, and there are **Great Horned and Barred Owls** in the denser woods. A **Peregrine** is a strong possibility in September.

The Ingonish River delta is a prime spot for **Belted Kingfisher** — I have seen as many as a dozen in the area in late summer — and flycatchers, with **Alder and Least Flycatchers** the most common representatives. **Mourning Warbler** is fairly common with a few **Nashville Warbler** in secondgrowth, while **Blackburnian and Baybreasted Warblers** are found in the taller trees bordering the road and river. Among the breeding species still present in early September are **Redwinged and Rusty Blackbirds, Scarlet Tanager and Purple Finch**. Most eastern sparrows, including **Sharptailed, Lincoln's and Swamp Sparrows**, linger here in fall.

Other places to visit from this site
Although it requires a long drive, the Cape North peninsula should be visited during the summer. St. Paul Island a few miles offshore has almost vertical 330 ft. cliffs which support a mixed colony of **Great and Doublecrested Cormorants**. Pelagics are also regular in these waters with large numbers of **Greater and Sooty Shearwaters** possible inshore in foggy conditions in summer. The same conditions in spring and early winter are likely to produce **Northern Fulmar and Leach's Storm-petrel**.

The wooded headland beyond Meat Cove and Capstick west of St. Lawrence Bay is an excellent place to look for **Osprey, Northern Goshawk and Merlin**, all of which nest. Owls are seldom seen or heard, although reports of migrant **Longeared Owl** are interesting considering their rarity in Cape Breton and absence in Newfoundland. **Boreal Owl** is more likely, but a **Snowy Owl** could be expected in winter. Most boreal songbirds occur here, with **Graycheeked Thrush, Mourning and Baybreasted Warblers, and Lincoln's Sparrow** particularly common. **Pine Grosbeak and Red Crossbill** are less regular in their appearances. Bay St. Lawrence is popular with a number of gulls, including **Iceland Gull** in winter, but there are very few visits here in summer.

Northern Shrike often make a landing here in mid October, but the best birding is to the south in the Sugar Loaf area. The road between Bay St. Lawrence and Cape North gives a good cross-section of breeding birds — I have totalled over 70 species in late June and early July. The small campground near Cabot's Landing has **Gray Catbird** in summer, and **Brown Thrasher and Northern Mockingbird** in late spring and mid fall, and the summer homes always have a few **Barn Swallow and Bobolink** staking out territories in summer. **Bank Swallow** colonies occupy two sand pits and a sandstone cliff, but the greatest attraction is the number of warblers that can be seen. **Tennessee, Blackpoll, Baybreasted, Palm and Mourning Warblers, Ovenbird and Northern Waterthrush** are all relatively common, and the shrubbery has a few **Chestnutsided and Wilson's Warblers** and the occasional **Philadelphia Vireo or Canada Warbler. Lincoln's Sparrow** rivals the more widespread **Whitethroated and Swamp Sparrows** alongside the road. Migration in May and October is marked by good numbers of **American Tree and Whitecrowned Sparrows** and a few **Water Pipit and Lapland Longspur.**

One of my favourite spots along this coast is South Pond which lies along Aspy Bay. This is a choice habitat for a wide variety of waterfowl and shorebirds, especially in fall. **Semipalmated Plover and Sanderling** prefer the outer sandy shore, but other species gather on the mudflats and saltmarshes. The first birds arrive in July and most have left by the end of September. **Blackbellied Plover, Least and Semipalmated Sandpipers** are common, and there have been a few **Pectoral and Western Sandpipers** with them. **Willet, Lesser Yellowlegs, Red Knot and Dunlin** are all possible. Marshbirds are apparently non-breeders, although late summer **Sora and Virginia Rail** could nest in the area. Gulls and terns at the sandbar tip usually include a few **Bonaparte's Gull** in September-early October, and **Black Tern** may be regular in spring and summer.

Waterfowl are very common on migration with dabbling ducks on the saltmarshes and diving ducks offshore. **Northern Pintail** are fairly common, and there have been several reports of **Mallard and American Wigeon**. The only nesting species appear to be **Ringnecked Duck and Redbreasted Merganser** judging by mid August family groups. Birds of prey regularly drop by on migration with **Peregrine** a holy terror for the **Greenwinged and Bluewinged Teal** from mid August to late September. **Sharpshinned Hawk and Merlin** have a good dinner menu with **Cedar Waxwing, Pine Grosbeak and Whitecrowned Sparrow** feeding in the dune grasses and thrushes and warblers plentiful in the woods. Wintering sparrows are a possibility since **Sharptailed Sparrows** are known to stay as late as the beginning of October.

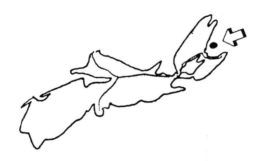

BIRD ISLANDS

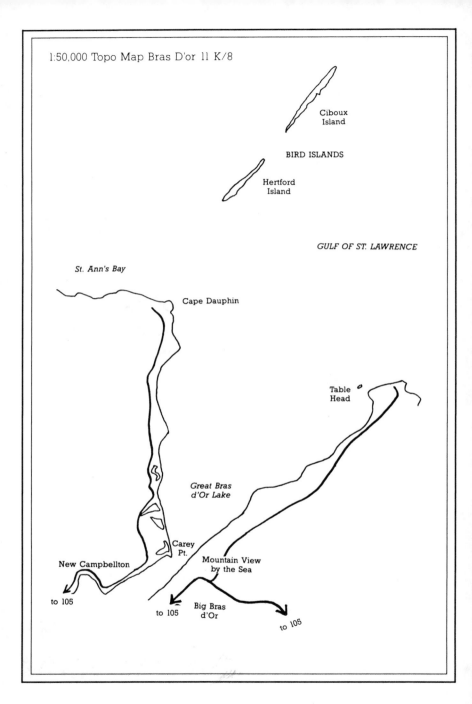

1:50,000 Topo Map Bras D'or 11 K/8

Ciboux
Island

BIRD ISLANDS

Hertford
Island

GULF OF ST. LAWRENCE

St. Ann's Bay

Cape Dauphin

Table
Head

*Great Bras
d'Or Lake*

Carey
Pt.

New Campbellton

Mountain View
by the Sea

to 105

to 105

Big Bras
d'Or

to 105

Victoria County is covered for the most part with coniferous forest and offers little in the way of farming opportunities, although there are farms in the Talbotvale-North River area where a **Great Gray Owl** was a recent surprise to local residents. Pioneer stands of hardwood have the greatest variety of species on migration, and mixed stands around Bras d'Or Lake the highest number of breeding species. The main feature is not on the land but a short distance out to sea north of Cape Dauphin, where two narrow rocky islands are jointly owned and protected by two government agencies and the Nova Scotia Bird Society.

The Bird Islands of Hertford and Ciboux have steep cliffs and grassy slopes with a number of colonial seabird species. Boat tours leave from Mountain View-by-the-Sea and last just over two hours. There is a regular schedule but special trips can be made by booking in advance — Captain Van Schaick will take birders out in the early morning when the birds are most active. The captain and his staff know the birds well and the trip is highly recommended since excellent views are possible of most species and of a herd of gray seals gathering off Ciboux Island in summer. Landings are discouraged — and are rarely possible, but the best views are from the water.

Razorbill

Numbers vary from year to year, but are apparently increasing. This is the only regular **Atlantic Puffin** colony in Cape Breton, and the number of **Blacklegged Kittiwake** has been steadily increasing since the first birds arrived in the 1970s. On an early July visit in 1981, I counted **80+ Atlantic Puffin nests, 160+ of Blacklegged Kittiwake, and 30 of Razorbill** — like the puffins they use tunnels in the rockface. I also saw **500+ Great and 200 Doublecrested Cormorants** in the mixed colony on Hertford Island, **25+ Black Guillemot, 26 Common** and a drake **King Eider** off Ciboux Island, and a few **Spotted Sandpiper**. Although rarely seen, there are also some **Leach's Storm-petrel** nesting on the islands, and shearwaters on rare occasions.

The arrival of the kittiwakes has meant the loss of the **Common and Arctic Tern** colonies—these have attracted Cape Breton's only **Roseate Tern**. The number of **Great Blackbacked and Herring Gulls** has, however, continued to grow—putting the alcids, especially puffins, under some predatory pressure. An occasional bird may fall to a passing **Peregrine or Gyrfalcon** in fall or a resident **Bald Eagle**. These have little to add to their regular fish diet in winter except **Purple Sandpiper** on the rocks.

The woods and old fields around Mountain View-by-the-Sea are worth checking out in summer as they contain a wide variety of nesting songbirds, including some species difficult to find elsewhere. A July visit yielded a good mix of boreal and hardwood species with high populations of **Boreal Chickadee, Redeyed Vireo, Black-and-white, Magnolia, Yellowrumped and Blackburnian Warblers, Darkeyed Junco, Whitethroated, Lincoln's and Song Sparrows**. The fields and shrubs by the landing also had **Veery, Mourning Warbler, Purple Finch and Fox Sparrow**. I suspect a few more visits would turn up some surprises, especially on the other side of the road where there is a cutover area. **Pileated Woodpecker and Broadwinged Hawk** are quite likely in this area, but **Bald Eagle and American Kestrel** are the usual nesting raptors. **Spotted Sandpiper** nest along the shores of Great Bras d'Or Lake, and there are a few plovers and sandpipers in fall.

Other places to visit from this site

The first good site driving south from Ingonish is the small park at North Shore. You can look out over the Gulf of St. Lawrence and see **Common Loon and Rednecked Grebe** staging in early fall. Some of these birds, plus a few **Redthroated Loon and Horned Grebe**, remain into early winter when seaducks and alcids are likely. The landscaped lawns and woods of North Shore have a number of nesting thrushes, warblers and sparrows, but they are best visited for the late summer flocks of **Pine Siskin and Whitewinged Crossbill—Common Redpoll** are less reliable. Breeding birds are joined by migrants in late summer, and later movements may turn up the regular **Bobolinks** and infrequent **Northern Oriole, Dickcissel and Scarlet Tanager**. There are also chances of finding **Bald Eagle, Osprey and Merlin** along this coastline in summer and **Gyrfalcon and Peregrine** in fall.

St. Ann's has a good mix of softwoods and hardwoods, and some good saltmarshes. The commonest waterbirds are **Great Blue Heron and Doublecrested Cormorant**—both nesting not too far away, but there have been visits by **Snowy Egret and Glossy Ibis** in spring and late summer. Gulls and terns are frequent sights on the small spits below Kelly's Mountain which offers an excellent view of the whole area. **Bald Eagle** is a common breeding species, and there are records of **Golden Eagle** in mid July and **Peregrine** in late September. **Pileated Woodpecker** can be heard, and sometimes seen, in the mixed woods on the mountain slopes. Kelly's Mountain feels much higher than it actually is, especially in winter when glare ice can be a major problem—there is a very sharp hairpin turn which should be taken at the posted speeds. I haven't driven it myself, but I suspect the road through New Campbellton to Cape Dauphin is worth taking. There are a number of small coastal ponds that look excellent for waterfowl, marshbirds and shorebirds in spring and fall.

Boularderie Island has been heavily logged, creating plenty of secondgrowth for a diversified avifauna. Boreal species are common with **Threetoed Woodpecker** almost certainly resident and **Pileated Woodpecker** very conspicuous. The most interesting summer and fall addition to the area is **Turkey Vulture** which rarely ventures this far north. The cutover areas have brought a number of rarer nesting species to the region, especially **Chestnutsided Warbler** but also **Bobolink, Scarlet Tanager and Rosebreasted Grosbeak**. A few ducks nest on Boularderie Island — the most interesting species not yet proven to breed is **Redhead** which has paired off in spring on several occasions with unknown results.

Point Aconi and Alder Point, accessible from either side of the Little Bras d'Or, offer a chance of seeing the colonial seabirds from the Bird Islands, especially **Great Cormorant** which also winter here in small numbers. Point Aconi is best reached by taking Exit 17 off Highway 105 and driving to the end of Highway 162 which leads nowhere in particular. A short walk up a slight slope leads to a rocky cliff offering a fine view of the Atlantic Ocean and Bird Islands. This is a good place to look for loons, seaducks and alcids in winter.

A number of **Northern Gannet** also pass by on onshore winds in late July and October. **Broadwinged and Redtailed Hawks** are quite likely in summer when the commonest raptors are **Bald Eagle and Osprey**. Shorebirds are common in fall with **Whimbrel and Willet** regular and **Buffbreasted Sandpiper** possible, and there are usually a few ducks and gulls. A mid July **Glaucous Gull** had no reason to be here, but then neither did a 1980 **Lawrence's Warbler**! Cottage development has cleared some of the original forest and produced new habitats for open country birds, especially **American Kestrel, Eastern Kingbird, Bobolink and Common Grackle**.

North Sydney lies a short drive to the south at the end of Highway 105. The ferry terminal and fishing provide most of the jobs here and offer a year-round bonus to the gulls. The winter months provide the best opportunity to pick up northern species. Large numbers of **Iceland Gull** hang around the fishplant with a few **Glaucous and Blackheaded Gulls**. This site has also brought a few **Ivory Gull** visits, and I suspect a **Sabine's Gull** would not be a surprise in a fall storm. Ducks are also common from late fall into winter, with **Harlequin and Barrow's Goldeneye** a fair reward for anyone brave enough to withstand the icy winds. Loons and alcids winter in the harbour unless the ice moves in, and there are always a few **Great Cormorant** parties flying around.

During the summer birding is more limited, but the ferries provide good opportunities to see **Greater, Sooty, Cory's and Manx Shearwaters** close to land in Sydney Harbour. **Great and Doublecrested Cormorants** are on the water with a few **Common Loon**, and both **Whitewinged Scoter and Black Guillemot** are regularly seen from the ferry. Nesting waterfowl include **Black Duck, Greenwinged and Bluewinged Teal and Common Merganser**. Summer is a good time to look for the many pairs of **Bald Eagle** nesting in the area, or the very local **Barred Owls** close to Sydney Mines.

Nearby Coxheath adds **Osprey, Broadwinged and Redtailed Hawks**, and a definite chance of adding **Cooper's Hawk, Northern Harrier and Shorteared Owl** over the marshes by Sydney River. There have also been a few herons here — the best being a summer **Blackcrowned Night Heron**. The tidal arms are very popular with **Blackheaded Gulls** which compete with **Belted Kingfisher** for small fish by the road and railway bridges. A drive to Sydney Forks could add a few species — there have been summer records of **Warbling Vireo and Prothonotary Warbler**, a mid August **Loggerhead Shrike**, and a **Yellowthroated Warbler** in mid December. **Yellowbellied Sapsucker, Blackbacked Woodpecker, Yellowbellied, Alder and Olivesided Flycatchers, Gray Jay, Brown Creeper, Solitary Vireo, Rosebreasted Grosbeak and Pine Siskin** all nest.

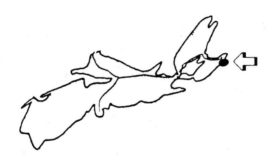

GLACE BAY AREA

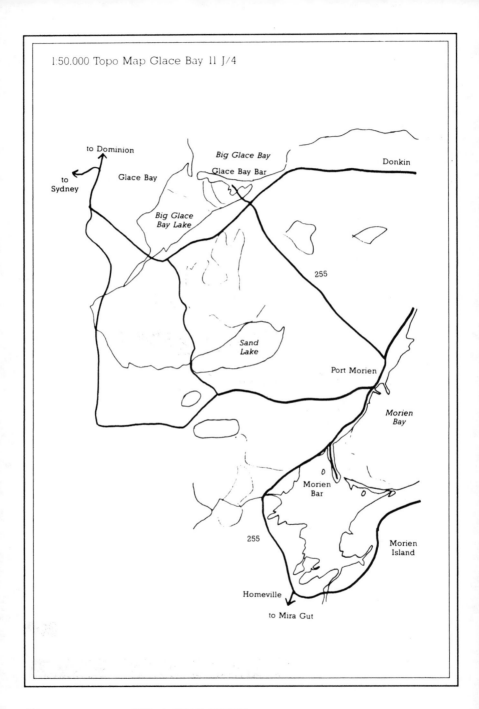

1:50,000 Topo Map Glace Bay 11 J/4

to Dominion

to Sydney

Glace Bay

Big Glace Bay

Glace Bay Bar

Donkin

Big Glace Bay Lake

255

Sand Lake

Port Morien

Morien Bay

Morien Bar

Morien Island

255

Homeville

to Mira Gut

This region has long been associated with coal mining and has some of the oldest and most famous mines in Nova Scotia. Glace Bay's mine has not been operating for some time, but the above-ground interpretive display, below-ground guided trips, and the miner's choir have combined to keep the cultural heritage intact. The Miner's Museum in Glace Bay opened in 1967, and the trip to coal seams under the Atlantic Ocean is an experience you never forget. The oldest coal mine is not at Glace Bay but at nearby Port Morien where the French started mining coal in 1720 — the spot is marked by a cairn. This is also the area where Rita MacNeil grew up which explains her most famous song — a tribute to the miners.

Birders have a choice of several excellent shorebird locations within easy reach and the Glace Bay Sanctuary which offers good birding year round. All the best sites are within five minutes of Glace Bay. A number of local birdwatchers maintained a local Cape Breton chapter of the Nova Scotia Bird Society and organized field trips for many years. Many of the founder members are no longer around, but Frank Robertson remains the only regular bird columnist in the province from his home in New Waterford.

The first site is Lingan Bar just north of Dominion. The long sandbar used to be connected to the New Waterford side of Lingan Bay by a bridge, but this has now gone and the only access is off the road from Lingan. Many maps now refer to this area as Dominion Beach which is the name of the provincial park designed to protect it from gravel extraction and heavy recreational use. The beach is only devoid of visitors in winter when a mid January **Lesser Scaup** and a late April **Snow Goose** were a change from the usual wintering and migrant **Greater Scaup**. As many as **180 Black Duck** gather here in November, but few remain through the winter.

Spring brings a small number of shorebirds, plus occasional landbirds — notably a **Whitewinged Dove** in late May. **Snowy Egrets** have also visited the bar in spring, but **Great Blue Heron** and an occasional **American Bittern** are more likely. **American Kestrel and Shorteared Owl** hunt along the dunes, but the most interesting breeding record was that of a **Northern Mockingbird** feeding a youngster by the snackbar. Youngsters of another kind were suitably impressed! A few parties of waterfowl call in around mid September, but few stay as hunting pressure is intense. Nevertheless, Lingan Bar holds the distinction of hosting **13 Gadwall** late in September — one of the largest flocks in the province so far. **Saw-whet Owls** also rest up here at times, perhaps drawn by the restless flocks of **Water Pipit, Horned Lark, Lapland Longspur, Snow Bunting** and sparrows.

The most obvious fall migrants are, however, shorebirds. Typical high counts are **100 Semipalmated Plover, 150 Blackbellied Plover, 50+ Greater Yellowlegs, 50 Least Sandpiper, 150 Semipalmated Sandpiper and 65 Sanderling.** Other species in smaller numbers are **25 Lesser Golden Plover, 22 Whimbrel, 16 Willet, 20 Shortbilled Dowitcher and 20 Dunlin.** Apart from regular **Hudsonian Godwit, Ruddy Turnstone, Red Knot, Lesser Yellowlegs and Whiterumped Sandpiper**, you can also try for **Piping Plover, Killdeer, Pectoral and Buffbreasted Sandpipers**. Most birds prefer the flats at low tide, but a few birds feed along the beach at high tide.

The second site is one of the best in Cape Breton, although the backdrop of a heavywater plant and its clouds of superheated steam do little to suggest that the waters and marshes of Big Glace Bay Lake are anything special. The road by the plant is sometimes closed — watch for the flashing lights, and you aren't allowed to park by the bridge. I have parked in the spacious lot by the plant and walked back to the bridge to check out the rafts of **Greater Scaup, Common and Redbreasted Margansers** which gather in late fall and winter — these birds are not always easy to see from the rest of the sanctuary. The best access is off the Donkin road opposite Highway 255 to Port Morien. A rough dirt road leads to the marshes and sand dunes of Glace Bay Bar — watch where you park because this is a public right-of-way.

These saltmarshes are an excellent place to see waterfowl, and nearly every eastern species has turned up here in reasonable numbers. A flock of about **1200 Canada Geese** spend their time here and at Morien Bar, and numbers build up in March when **Brant** are possible. There may also be **300 Greater Scaup** and slightly smaller numbers of **Black Duck, Common Goldeneye, Common and Redbreasted Mergansers** from late fall on. **Eurasian Wigeon, Ringnecked Duck and Bufflehead** have also braved the chilly winds that blow over the lake, and a **Tundra Swan** made it through with flying colours. Winter is also a good time to look over the gull flocks, which include over **50**, sometimes **100, Blackheaded Gull. Ivory and Little Gulls** have both been seen after the migrant **Bonaparte's Gulls** have left, and there are usually a few **Blacklegged Kittiwake** in the bay with wintering **Iceland Gulls. Common Murre and Dovekie**, and the odd **Barrow's Goldeneye or Thickbilled Murre**, can be looked for on Big Glace Bay from the shelter of a beach ridge of sand and pebbles, where flocks of **Snow Bunting** usually contain a few **Lapland Longspur**. A few **Brownheaded Cowbird, American Tree, Fox and Song Sparrows** may join them, although most overwintering songbirds prefer to settle in at feeders.

Spring brings a rush of waterfowl to the ponds and marshes. **Piedbilled and Horned Grebes** appear with the first returning ducks in early April to May, when the flocks of **Black Duck, Greenwinged and Bluewinged Teal** may contain a few **Mallard, Northern Pintail, Gadwall, American Wigeon and Lesser Scaup**. There have even been **Eurasian Wigeon** on a more or less regular basis in spring. **Black Duck, Greenwinged and Bluewinged Teal** nest in small numbers, and there are enough summering **Mallard and American Wigeon** to suggest they do, too. Resident **Bald Eagle and Great Horned Owl** dispose of a few ducklings, and the odd **Snowy or Shorteared Owl** in spring take one or two. A walk through the wet grass may disturb a **Snowy Egret**, or one of the nesting pairs of **American Bittern**. You don't have to walk far to disturb the breeding **Willet** — they take to noisy flight as soon as you put a foot in their marsh. **Purple Martin** occasionally join the swallows hawking over the water, and **Brown Thrasher and Dickcissel** have turned up in the scrub and grasses on the south side of the lake.

Fall offers a greater variety of species, including some rare migrants. The first rush is usually of shorebirds in early August. While not particularly numerous, the flats should be carefully scanned at low tide for **Hudsonian Godwit** — as many as **70** were counted one day in mid August. Roosting flocks often gather on the upper beaches at high tide, and I have seen **Pectoral and Buffbreasted Sandpipers** among the **Blackbellied Plover** parties. A few **Greater Yellowlegs, Whiterumped Sandpiper and Dunlin** are tempted into staying well into November when most birds have had the good sense to leave. Marshbirds are not seen as often as in spring, but **American Coot and Glossy Ibis** are fairly regular, and a **Yellow Rail** appeared one fall.

After September the waterfowl and gulls take over. **Horned Grebe** numbers build on the bay while a few **Piedbilled Grebe** check out the brackish waters of the lake. As many as **16 Gadwall** have been counted in late September, and the frosts of October have not deterred **Snow Goose, American Wigeon and Northern Shoveler. Bonaparte's Gulls** often feed close to the heavywater plant settling tanks, and there are usually a few **Ringbilled Gull** until October. Most of the terns seen here are **Arctic Tern**, but an odd **Caspian Tern** may appear — any late tern should be checked out as a possible **Forster's Tern** which visits Atlantic Canada in November and December. Boreal species provide the bulk of the songbirds in fall and early winter, but rarer strays have included **Northern Mockingbird, Brown Thrasher, Bluegray Gnatcatcher and Warbling Vireo**, as well as the regular **Dickcissels**. **Bohemian Waxwing** flocks may fly in to snatch some unclaimed berries after going the rounds in New Waterford and Glace Bay (their presence may have something to do with Cape Breton College!)

Another excellent birding site is found by following Highway 255 to Port Morien and then driving another 2 miles south to a sandbar pointing south. A rough road takes you out to a gravel parking lot where there is a snackbar in summer. Because picnickers and clamdiggers are apt to arrive early if the tide is out, it is best to time your visit even earlier or in late afternoon at low tide. A telescope is a handy aid as the birds spread out over the mud flats all the way to Homeville. At high tide the birds roost on Morien Island, but a loop round to Homeville and then about 3 miles onto Morien Island and along the complementary sandbar will reveal most species.

My highest July-August counts of the commoner species are **115 Semipalmated Plover, 85 Blackbellied Plover, 25 Ruddy Turnstone, 18 Spotted Sandpiper, 17 Willet, 50 Greater and 20 Lesser Yellowlegs, 120 Whiterumped Sandpiper, 81 Shortbilled Dowitcher, 20 Least Sandpiper, 220 Semipalmated Sandpiper, 15 Hudsonian Godwit and 35 Sanderling**. A few **Whimbrel, Red Knot, Dunlin and Pectoral Sandpiper** also appear at this time. By September most of the birds are leaving, but counts of **40 Semipalmated Plover, 50 Blackbellied Plover, 27 Greater Yellowlegs, 44 Red Knot, 38 Whiterumped Sandpiper, 50 Dunlin, 8 Shortbilled Dowitcher, 25 Semipalmated Sandpiper, 35 Sanderling and a Buffbreasted Sandpiper** indicate the attractiveness of the marshes. Others have seen **Piping Plover, Killdeer and Lesser Golden Plover** in mid September and early October. On my late October visits, only **Blackbellied Plover and Greater Yellowlegs** came close to double figures.

Gulls and terns are present in good numbers, especially when the tide is on the turn and small fish are on the move — it's not unusual to see **hundreds** of both **Arctic and Common Terns. Laughing Gull and Black Tern** are regular in spring and early summer. Marshbirds are also common. I have counted over **60 Great Blue Heron** strung out over the flats at low tide, and local residents have reported **Yellowcrowned and**

Blackcrowned Night Herons, Snowy and Great Egrets, and Glossy Ibis both here and on the adjoining part of Morien Island in late summer and early fall. These may be scattered by the **Bald Eagle and Osprey** fishing the deeper waters. **Northern Harrier and Shorteared Owl** both patrol the sandbars when the crowds are gone. **Roughlegged Hawk** is a common sight in spring, and **Peregrine, Merlin and American Kestrel** appear in both spring and fall. Morien Island has a few summering **Redtailed Hawks**, but they rarely stray over to the saltmarshes.

Waterfowl are also common both outside and inside the bar. **Common and Redthroated Loons** can be looked for in the deeper water and in the channel between the two bars, and there are always a few **Great Cormorant** near Port Morien. Diving ducks are also common — **500+ Whitewinged Scoter** have been counted in late June, and **Hooded Merganser** is fairly regular. But geese and dabbling ducks steal most of the limelight. As many as **4000 Canada Geese and 300 Black Duck** stage here in spring and fall, and the flocks may contain **Brant and Snow Geese. Mallard, Northern Pintail, American Wigeon, Greenwinged and Bluewinged Teal** are all found with the excitable parties of **Black Duck**. While songbirds should not be expected to take to this desolate beach with its notable lack of cover, early winter parties of **Horned Lark, Snow Bunting and Lapland Longspur** do swirl over the marshes and dunes with a few late **Savannah Sparrow**. That some stay is indicated by a count of **50+ Lapland Longspur** in mid February.

The quiet marsh on the other side of the mudflats is a pleasant change from the noise on the Morien Bar side. The silence is broken by the anguished squeals of nesting **Willet** and the harsh rattle of several pairs of **Belted Kingfisher. Great Blue Heron, Great and Doublecrested Cormorants** go about their business silently, and the marsh should be checked for rarer visitors. **Snowy Egret and Glossy Ibis** are often found in spring, and **Caspian Terns** sometimes roost with the gulls on the bar. A **Common Redshank** reported here one August was more likely to have been a **Spotted Redshank**. The Loyalist Church grounds offer a good view of the marshes.

Great Horned Owls pretty much have the area to themselves, although a **Northern Harrier or Shorteared Owl** may glide over, but an early January **Boreal Owl** suggests that other eyes are watching the shrubbery. Large numbers of thrushes, warblers and sparrows pass through here, and there are **Bobolink** in the bushes from May to September. **Ringnecked Pheasant** nests here, although **Ruffed Grouse** is more likely in the woods.

Other places to visit from this area

Although Sydney's sulphurous smoke coats everything with an orange glow, there is little in the birdlife to make it shine. The wide stretches of the Sydney River have ducks and gulls year round. **Common Loon, Great and Doublecrested Cormorants, Greenwinged Teal and Common Goldeneye** are joined in fall by the wintering **Greater Scaup and Oldsquaw**, but you should be careful of checking off **Mallard** with the wild **Black Duck** parties, especially by Wentworth Park where there is a feral flock. The wild birds are noticeably large and locally known as "Labrador Blacks" — they are also prized table birds! The marshes by Southwest Arm are more likely to draw marshbirds, which have included **Purple Gallinule** in early February and **Yellowcrowned Night Heron** in early August. Shorebirds are less frequent, but a **Spotted Sandpiper** found the marshes attractive enough to stay into November.

Bald Eagle and Osprey are often seen close to town, and a **Broadwinged Hawk** took on the daunting task of trying to overwinter. **Redtailed Hawk and American Kestrel** are much more likely to make it through. The wintering gulls, which include good numbers of **Glaucous and Iceland Gulls**, share the lugubrious surroundings of the slag heap to the north of the city with a large roost of **Common Raven**. Rather more appealing is the migration of up to **200 Common Nighthawk** along the river in August and early September. This aerial traffic jam is nothing compared to what can be seen on the city streets — make sure your insurance policy is paid up as many local drivers don't have any insurance!

Patches of alders and softwoods within city limits are good places to look for parties of **Pine Siskin and Common Redpoll** in winter, as well as flocks of **American Tree Sparrow, Evening and Pine Grosbeaks, Red and Whitewinged Crossbills**. Large flocks of **American Robin, Darkeyed Junco, Chipping and Song Sparrows** dwindle down to a precious few in winter when there may be a few **Bohemian Waxwing** (Cape Breton College is located here!) and **Northern Mockingbird. Northern Oriole** is the commonest of the rarer fall songbirds, which have included **Warbling Vireo, Orangecrowned and Cerulean Warblers, Yellowbreasted Chat, Dickcissel and Vesper Sparrow. Common Grackle** are common in the winter months, but the few **Northern Oriole** that resort to feeders rarely last beyond the middle of January.

The best birding around Sydney is at South Bar a few miles to the north off Highway 28. The North Sydney ferry terminal is visible across Sydney Harbour and so are several groups of **Great and Doublecrested Cormorants** drying their wings on the buoys. Wintering waterfowl can be observed from the end of the mile-long semicircular sand and pebble spit. **Oldsquaw** is the commonest wintering species, but **Greater Scaup, Common Goldeneye, Whitewinged, Black and Surf Scoters, and Common Eider** are all probable, and **Hooded Merganser** is also possible among the **Common and Redbreasted Mergansers**. Very few dabbling ducks use the spit because of hunting pressure.

The main late summer-early fall attraction is the concentration of shorebirds. A walk along the bar any time between late July and early September will flush up more than a dozen species, and this is one of the few sites providing a good roosting location at high tide. At least **2 Curlew Sandpiper** have been reported in early October, and the potential of the bar is very high. The best time to visit is on a rising or falling tide when the birds are actively feeding, but high tide offers the chance of counting birds in tight flocks near the light.

A visit I made in early August with the tide on the ebb is typical of what can be expected of South Bar. I spent three hours here and noted **72 Semipalmated Plover, 54 Ruddy Turnstone, 62 Greater Yellowlegs, 37+ Lesser Yellowlegs, 11 Spotted and Whiterumped Sandpipers, and 320+ Semipalmated Sandpiper**. There were also a few **Blackbellied Plover, Willet, Least Sandpiper and Sanderling** and a single **Buffbreasted Sandpiper. Red Knot and Dunlin** are present in small numbers with the immature **Whiterumped Sandpipers** in October and early November, and a few hardy individuals may linger into winter. There are usually a few **Great Blue Heron** on the mudflats at low tide, so a rarer egret or heron should not be unexpected. An assortment of **Horned Lark and Lapland Longspur** temporarily join the wintering **Snow Bunting** flocks in early winter, and any immature birds should be carefully examined as the first Cape Breton **Northern Wheatear** was noted here in the 1970s.

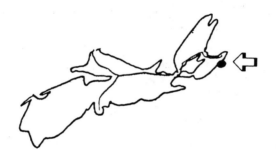

LOUISBOURG

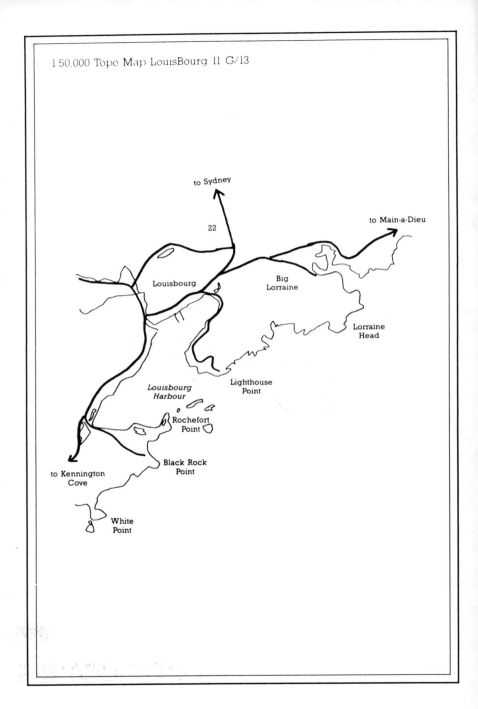

1 50,000 Topo Map LouisBourg 11 G/13

to Sydney

22

Louisbourg

to Main-a-Dieu

Big
Lorraine

Lorraine
Head

Lighthouse
Point

*Louisbourg
Harbour*

Rochefort
Point

Black Rock
Point

to Kennington
Cove

White
Point

The French picked the wrong place to build their "impregnable" fortress in the 1700s. What they apparently overlooked were the heavy mists and thick fog that blanket this area when everywhere else is bathing in sunshine. I worked two summers at the reconstructed fortress, and I must admit there were days that you couldn't see the modern town of Louisbourg at all. On the plus side, the fog usually lifts from the surrounding countryside long before it leaves the harbour—one reason why this is a popular holiday area. Farming is also widespread in the Marion Bridge area—immortalized in local folksongs.

The Mira River is more like a lake than a river, and it offers a contrast to the barren wastes and boreal forests of Louisbourg. While Louisbourg itself has a strong French flavour, the modern town and many of the smaller communities typify the Scottish influence. There is an excellent Seaquarium of the Atlantic in Louisbourg—designed and operated by Alex Storm who had a lot to do with the early exploration of the harbour and salvage operations. Most people pass through on their way to the Fortress, but if you don't fancy the period meals and hard bread of the reconstructed site try stopping in Louisbourg for a meal.

The town is a good place to bird, especially if the fishplant is operating. In winter there are **hundreds of Iceland Gull** which arrive in late October and stay until May with a few **Glaucous and Blackheaded Gulls**. Waterfowl and alcids also spend the winter in the ice-free harbour. **Common Loon** is certainly common here, but the **Redthroated Loon, Rednecked and Horned Grebes** so prominent in November rarely stay. **Common Goldeneye and Oldsquaw** flocks invariably contain a few **Barrow's Goldeneye**, and the **Black Guillemots** are joined by **Dovekie, Thickbilled and Common Murres**. An early winter **Ruddy Duck** looked a little out of place, but no more than a flock of **Glossy Ibis** which spent part of one spring and summer dodging dogs and children. They fared pretty well, and so do the wintering **Ruddy Turnstone** which spend their time between the saltmarsh beach and the stream at the east end of town. Shorebirds of all kinds like this area and so did a mid August **Least Tern** and an early September **Piedbilled Grebe**.

The town is also a good place to look for landbirds—I enjoyed my walks around the community which turned some good species, although I missed more than I saw! A number of local residents have operated feeders over the years and these have attracted a bewildering array of rarities, including **Prothonotary Warbler, Yellowbreasted**

Chat, Yellowheaded Blackbird, Dickcissel and Lark Sparrow. My modest collection of **50 Evening Grosbeak, 25 Purple Finch, Red and Whitewinged Crossbills, American Goldfinch, Pine Siskin, Common Redpoll, Darkeyed Junco, Fox and Whitethroated Sparrows** pales by comparison, but I did have a **Cooper's Hawk** lording it over the **Sharpshinned Hawks** that normally lay claim to the feeders. **Northern Shrike** is another possible predator, although most birds do not wander into town. **Western Kingbird and Northern Mockingbird** are both regular winter species, but **Scarlet Tanager** is much more likely in spring, when the returning birds of prey include a good number of **American Kestrel and Merlin**. The most interesting spring raptor was a **Turkey Vulture** drifting lazily in on a front.

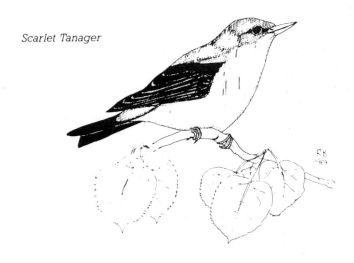

Scarlet Tanager

Fortress of Louisbourg National Historic Park is really two parks in one — the reconstructed site and the natural area which is much larger in size but largely unknown to the average tourist. The 55 acres of the site are dominated by the buildings — many of them rebuilt using the original plans. The story is told in the visitor centre atop one of the knolls overlooking the site. Buses transport visitors to the site, which takes about three hours to really experience. A visiting birder should make two visits — one for the history and one for the natural history.

In summer the eaves offer nesting sites to **Cliff and Barn Swallows**, while yards and fields support **American Robin, Savannah and Song Sparrows**. A visit outside the summer season will add migrant thrushes, warblers, **Water Pipit and Bobolink** in the early fall, and flocks of **Horned Lark, Lapland Longspur and Snow Bunting** later on. I found a **Yellowbreasted Chat** sheltering in one of the doorways in early winter, and there is an old record of a **Fieldfare** in winter. The shoreline between Louisbourg and the Royal Battery offers good views of the harbour. **Redthroated Loon, Rednecked and Horned Grebes** are all fairly common in early winter, when the first wintering flocks of **Common Goldeneye and Oldsquaw** start to build up. These flocks, with their attendant **Barrow's Goldeneye**, and most of the scoters and alcids are best viewed from the shoreline between the site and the small barachois pond below the Dauphine Gate.

This location has a wintering flock of **75+ Purple Sandpiper** and a few late **Red Knot, Whiterumped Sandpiper and Dunlin** at low tide. Earlier in the fall it is popular with other shorebirds, including occasional **Willet and Lesser Golden Plover**. The scrubby conifers and weedy fields have good numbers of **Redwinged and Rusty Blackbirds, and Bobolinks** in early fall. A few rare migrants always turn up along park roads—I have seen a **Great Crested Flycatcher** in late summer, and you can see **Eastern Phoebe** in the most unlikely places by the shore. The barachois pond has a nesting colony of **Arctic Tern** and summering **Doublecrested Cormorant**, but the best birds are the **30+ Surf Scoter** that gather on it in late September and October.

Perhaps the best birding is along the sand and pebble ridge leading to Rochefort Point. Approached from the site along the seawall or by an old gravel road extending beyond Rue Royale, this is a good spot to look for pelagics, especially **Northern Gannet**. **Piedbilled Grebe and American Coot** can be expected inshore in fall, when a few ducks and shorebirds rest along the muddy and rocky margins and are put to flight by tourists, red foxes or birds of prey. **Whimbrel** are regular visitors as they are all along the coast, and **Glossy Ibis** was a spring vagrant. Even rarer was a drake **Eurasian Wigeon** with a party of **Northern Pintail** in early winter. **Common Eider and Oldsquaw** flash white, black and brown in the breaking surf, and most of the black shadows flying by are **Great Cormorant**.

A little further along the shore between Black Rock and White Points, shorebirds are common on the pebble beaches and along the sandy margins. **Blackbellied Plover, Ruddy Turnstone, Dunlin, Whiterumped and Semipalmated Sandpipers** form the majority of the flocks, but **Willet** are present in July and August and may breed. **Whimbrel, Lesser Golden Plover, Killdeer, Red Knot and Buffbreasted Sandpiper** can all be looked for on the barrens. Passing **Peregrines** put the flocks to flight—there is nothing more thrilling than a falcon flat out after shorebirds. **Turkey Vulture and Cooper's Hawk** have both been seen arriving on warm fronts in spring, but there is nothing warm about winter when **Roughlegged Hawk** outnumber the few remaining **Redtailed Hawk**. Owls are a strong possibility on any visit with nesting **Barred Owl** probably joined by **Sawwhet and Boreal Owls** and infrequent migrant **Snowy, Longeared and Shorteared Owls**. The interior of the park is not well known, but both **Spruce Grouse and Blackbacked Woodpecker** have been seen on a number of occasions and may be quite common.

The road to Kennington Cove is open most of the year, although a detour is required during the summer when its sandy beach is filled with local residents and tourists. By mid September, the tourists have left and the cove is open for ducks. Small flocks of **Common Eider and Common Goldeneye** are joined by a few **Barrow's Goldeneye, Harlequin, Whitewinged and Surf Scoters**, and the winds generally keep them close to shore in the pounding surf. **Glaucous and Bonaparte's Gulls** have been seen here, and pelagics may be blown inshore—I have found dead **Leach's Storm-petrels** on the beach in October.

The coniferous woods and bogs by the road have a wide variety of breeding birds, with warblers the most conspicuous in midsummer—**Magnolia, Yellowrumped and Blackpoll Warblers** are all common. Most boreal birds are found, including **Spruce Grouse, Blackbacked Woodpecker and Red Crossbill**. The boggy ponds have a few **Black Duck and Greenwinged Teal**, and there are **Common Snipe**, and probably **Greater Yellowlegs**, on the bogs, but the interior of the park remains largely unexplored and unknown. **Northern Harrier** is fairly conspicuous in summer when **Red-**

tailed Hawk and Great Horned Owl are seen, but the status of **Sharpshinned Hawk, Merlin and American Kestrel** remains uncertain. **Osprey** is the only bird of prey regularly seen at Kennington Cove itself.

Other places to visit from this site

The coastal woods along Mira Bay have a few of the commoner boreal species such as **Pine Grosbeak and Fox Sparrow**, but the cliffs and rock/sand beaches dominate. The largest **Great Cormorant** colony on the Cape Breton coast is found here, and there are always a few **Common Loon** from late July when they leave their interior nesting ponds. **Redthroated Loon, Rednecked and Horned Grebes** arrive for a brief stay in late September. Marshbirds also like this area. **American Coot** are regular, and **Yellowcrowned Night Heron, Snowy Egret and Glossy Ibis** appear in late spring or early summer. **American Bittern** nests, and so does **Willet**, but shorebirds are few and far between. **Whimbrel** are common on the barrens from late July to early September, and they are followed by small numbers of **Lesser Golden Plover. Whiterumped Sandpiper** flocks pass through in October, but the only birds after this are the wintering **Purple Sandpipers**.

Some ducks, including **Gadwall**, stay for a month into October, but there are few ducks offshore until **Whitewinged Scoter** arrive with the returning **Great Cormorants** in late March. **Cliff Swallow** is a common sight among other hirundines, and **Purple Martin** regular enough to indicate nests in the future. I haven't birded this area enough to comment on the nesting songbirds, but I do know **Snow Bunting and Lapland Longspur** are common fall migrants.

You can't beat Mira River Provincial Park for a contrast from the boreal fare offered up by Louisbourg. The 140-site campground is a good place to stay to explore the hardwoods and secondgrowth that sets this area apart. Midweek and offseason visits are recommended because the park is extremely popular on summer weekends. **Bald Eagle and Osprey** both nest, and there are large numbers of **Doublecrested Cormorant** fishing the waters. **American Kestrel and Belted Kingfisher** dispute the use of lookout posts along Highway 22 from May to early October when the wintering kingfishers finally win out.

Ringnecked Pheasant is known to winter here and probably breeds, but early fall **Saw-whet Owls** are likely transients. **Great Horned Owl and Redtailed Hawk** certainly nest and can sometimes be seen with young in June or July. A few **Common Loon and Black Duck** take advantage of the lakelike expanses of the Mira River, and a pair of **Greater Scaup** were tempted into staying into mid June. The park's hardwoods have the greatest variety in late spring, and there are a number of rarer nesting species. **Solitary Vireo, Rosebreasted Grosbeak** and a selection of less common warblers are regular here — **Wood Thrush, Canada Warbler and Scarlet Tanager** are more likely strays destined to sing their hearts out to no avail. Huge flocks of **Tree Swallow** spread out over the lake in late summer, and these flocks usually have a few **Barn, Cliff and Bank Swallows**.

Another site I know to be productive is located southwest of Louisbourg off Highway 327. Gabarus Bay is well known to local hunters as a place to find waterfowl, especially **Northern Pintail, Oldsquaw and Common Eider. American Coot** are surprisingly common in fall, and all three scoters can be seen in September and October. There is a small colony of **Great Cormorant and Blacklegged Kittiwake** at Green Island off

Gabarus, and this is a good place to look for nonbreeding **Atlantic Puffin** and other alcids. **Northern Gannet** is to be expected, but shearwaters and jaegers may veer towards the Cape.

My only birding is at Belfry Lake, but it was almost a very expensive experience. My car spent two hours stuck axle-deep in the soft sand and shingle lining the shore as the tide rose. Only a helpful gravel extractor operator saved the day by towing my car out. Pelagics and shorebirds are common here, especially from late July to early October. **Red and Rednecked Phalaropes** are more likely than anywhere else in Cape Breton, and **Buffbreasted Sandpiper** may well be regular among the flocks of **Black-bellied and Lesser Golden Plovers**. Later in the fall **Whiterumped Sandpiper and Dunlin** dominate.

Just beyond Belfry Lake, Framboise Cove is an excellent area for waterfowl and stray marshbirds. It's well off the beaten track, but the number of **Great Egret** records suggests it has a lot to offer. **American Coot** are also found from late October to early December, just after the large rafts of **Greater Scaup**, and smaller numbers of **Black Scoter and Redthroated Loon**, leave, but during the buildup of wintering ducks other species can be looked for, including **Harlequin**. The sand and shingle beaches are favoured by **Sanderling**, and there has been a **Stilt Sandpiper** with the more regular **Willets**. An immature **Forster's Tern** in late October could have arrived in a storm. The beaches are also a good spot for grass-loving songbirds, as fall **Vesper and Grasshopper Sparrows** indicate. **Snow Buntings** are extremely common in winter.

In June I found an excellent short trail for boreal species along the road to Evans Island on the southern shore of the Bras d'Or. Located about two miles from Highway 4, a rather wet trail leads by the shoreline and up through spruce-fir-larch-birch woods to a grassy meadow. On a 90-minute stroll I tallied an impressive 31 species, including **Bald Eagle, Northern Goshawk, Spruce Grouse**, a family party of **Gray Jay, Boreal Chickadee, Gray-cheeked Thrush, Veery, Solitary Vireo and Baybreasted Warbler**. The commonest songbirds were **American Robin, Rubycrowned Kinglet, Magnolia Warbler, Common Yellowthroat, American Redstart and Whitethroated Sparrow**.

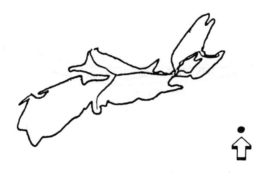

SABLE ISLAND

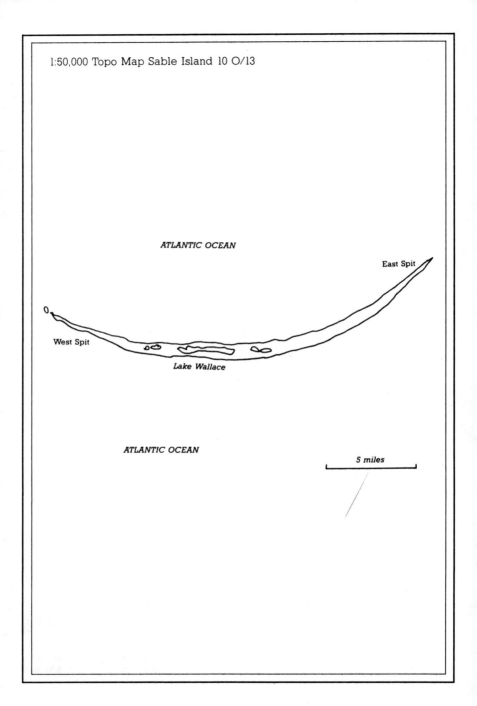

1:50,000 Topo Map Sable Island 10 O/13

ATLANTIC OCEAN

East Spit

0

West Spit

Lake Wallace

ATLANTIC OCEAN

5 miles

SABLE ISLAND

Whereas Seal Island is easily accessible from mainland Nova Scotia and Brier Island is an extension of it, the third mecca for birders — Sable Island — is stuck well beyond the reach of most visitors. Its offshore location makes it a natural trap for any birds that have strayed from their normal migration routes — the sudden appearance of this mid-ocean sandbar must change a lot of travel plans. Sable Island has a number of rarer birds year round, and it even had its own endemic species — the **Ipswich Sparrow**, until this sandy-coloured bird sealed its own taxonomic fate by consorting with mainland **Savannah Sparrows** on the beaches of Martinique and elsewhere. As many as **2000 pairs** still nest here, but the lure of greener grasses was obviously too much for a few migrants.

Storms change the shape, and even the position, of the island, but they do bring in unexpected vagrants. The same vagaries of the weather play havoc with the best-laid plans of birders who would like to arrive the same time as the birds. There is no regular flight schedule and few seats available on government supply aircraft, so landings and departures are a question of luck and patience. Anyone planning a visit is advised to keep in constant touch with the transportation source involved — on a daily basis if need be close to departure time.

Winter is not the time to savour Sable Island, but winter storms do bring "wrecks" and deposit migrants that should be far to the south and east. Food is very scarce, but a few **Ipswich Sparrows** do survive. **Northern Fulmar and Mew Gull** probably find enough food to sustain them, but the fate of midwinter **Killdeer, Boreal Owl, Blackpoll Warbler and Rusty Blackbird** would appear much less secure. Spring starts early, as visitors in mid March and early April have found. The first storms can be highly productive with winter birds like **Roughlegged Hawk, Pomarine Jaeger, Ivory and Mew Gulls** caught in the company of **Little Blue Heron, Wilson's Plover**, and a few early warblers and buntings. April is the time to look for some northbound **Piping Plover, Whimbrel and Shortbilled Dowitcher** and vagrant **Blue Grosbeak**.

By May the variety of birds on the island is greater than anywhere on the mainland. A few early pelagics appear in early May, although most **Wilson's Storm-petrel and Manx Shearwater** visits are somewhat later. Southern herons appear in May, with **Greenbacked and Little Blue Herons** regular, and **Glossy Ibis, Blackcrowned and Yellowcrowned Night Herons** less often seen. Most ducks pass by here, and a few **Northern Pintail, Gadwall, Wood and Ruddy Ducks** arrive close enough to the breeding season to consider nesting — the absence of aerial and land predators being a distinct advantage.

Shorebirds continue to stream through in small numbers, the more unusual sightings being **Marbled Godwit, Upland Sandpiper, Ruff and Wilson's Phalarope**. **Dovekie** linger in these waters to mid May when the first summer terns, including a few **Roseate** and occasional **Least Terns**, arrive. Among the landbirds, **Whip-poor-will** are irregular, **Roughwinged Swallow** infrequent, and **Cave Swallow and Acadian Flycatcher** interesting surprise migrants. Other May visitors include **Wood Thrush, Wormeating, Cerulean, Hermit and Hooded Warblers, Louisiana Waterthrush** and a number of fringillids, notably **Blue Grosbeak, Indigo Bunting and Field Sparrow**.

It's hard to judge when spring migration ends and fall migration begins on Sable Island — there may be northbound migrants at the same time as post-breeding adults are returning. June is the time to look for the greatest concentration of pelagics anywhere in the Atlantic Ocean. **Sooty Shearwater** may number in the **thousands**, and **Greater Shearwater** stream by in unending numbers, along with good numbers of **Northern Fulmar and Wilson's Storm-petrel. Cory's and Manx Shearwaters** are both regular visitors after the last of the breeding **Leach's Storm-petrels** have returned to their Atlantic colonies.

Purple Gallinule has made some unexpected summer visits here, as have early returning **Upland Sandpiper and Shortbilled Dowitcher**, but the commonest shorebird is the **Least Sandpiper** which finds enough to choose Sable Island as a regular nesting site. **Common, Arctic and Roseate Terns** all breed and have to contend with visiting **Pomarine and Parasitic Jaegers** and the odd **Great or South Polar Skua. Iceland Gulls** linger into summer when they provide an interesting contrast to their relatives from all over. **Laughing Gull and Sooty Tern** from the south and **Franklin's Gull** from the west are just as likely as ocean-wandering **Blacklegged Kittiwake** and immigrant **Little Gull**.

Sable Island is a meeting point for landbirds from all over the continent, too. **Blackbilled and Yellowbilled Cuckoos** regularly appear in summer and probably wonder where the trees and thus their caterpillar food have disappeared to. Northern-breeding **Northern Wheatear, Orangecrowned and Cape May Warblers, Pine Siskin and Common Redpoll** have shared the grasses with southern strays like **Hooded Warbler, Dickcissel and Orchard Oriole** and exotics like **Cave Swallow, Townsend's Warbler and Greentailed Towhee**.

Fall migration starts soon after the last spring migrants have left, and there may be only a few days between the last of the northbound warblers and the first of the southbound shorebirds. The four-week period beginning in mid July is dominated by shorebirds, especially the earlier-leaving species. **Upland and Stilt Sandpipers** have been noted at the same time as a few post-breeding herons, including **Yellowcrowned Night and Tricolored Herons. Franklin's Gull** is another late summer possibility, and **Black, Least and Royal Terns** have all appeared at this time. Landbirds are less numerous, but **Blackbilled Cuckoo** often reappear in July, along with **Northern Mockingbird, Wood Thrush, Louisiana Waterthrush, Prairie, Prothonotary and Hooded Warblers** — probably all the result of misdirected spring migration earlier. The peak of the shorebird and warbler migrations takes place from mid August to mid September when most birders visit.

Pelagics can number in **tens of thousands**, especially **Greater and Sooty Shearwaters**. Increasing numbers of **Cory's and Manx Shearwaters** are now showing up, and there is a faint hope of spotting both **Little and Audubon's Shearwaters**. Gulls are just as regular with parties of **Bonaparte's Gull** joined by a few **Franklin's, Little and Sabine's Gulls**. The large flocks of **Blacklegged Kittiwake** passing by in August and early September naturally attract the attention of **Pomarine and Parasitic Jaegers**. There are also a few **Longtailed Jaeger, Black and Roseate Terns** at this time, and the last of the summering **Caspian Terns**.

Herons regularly wander here into September. **Least Bittern and Tricolored Heron** have both been noted, although **Blackcrowned and Yellowcrowned Night Herons, Greenbacked and Little Blue Herons, Great, Cattle and Snowy Egrets** are more regular. **Sora and Virginia Rail** both wing by, as do occasional **Common Moorhen** and rarer rails. Shorebirds continue to be well represented by the various plovers and sandpipers. **Longbilled Dowitcher** is as common here as anywhere in Atlantic Canada, and there have been visits from **Marbled Godwit, Ruff, Buffbreasted, Baird's, Curlew and Western Sandpipers** during the peak shorebird migration. **Red and Rednecked Phalaropes** are common in these waters in late August, although numbers may not be as high as in the Bay of Fundy.

Songbirds pick up in late August, and almost any species can be looked for in the right weather conditions. While warblers and vireos provide the main interest, **Great Crested Flycatcher, Northern Mockingbird, Wood and Graycheeked Thrushes, Orchard Oriole and Yellowheaded Blackbird** have all been seen. Quite recently, Sable Island hosted a **Whitewinged Dove** — one of several that appeared in the Maritimes. Of species considered rare in Atlantic Canada, **Prothonotary, Prairie, Pine and Hooded Warblers, Yellowbreasted Chat, Kentucky and Connecticut Warblers** have all been seen in early September, and so have **Summer Tanager, Rufous-sided Towhee and Lark Sparrow** on a more regular basis.

Late fall sees the end of the shorebird and warbler migrations, and rather more waterfowl and thrushes than earlier on. However, there are always birds making a late start south or getting caught up in tropical disturbances. **Great and Snowy Egrets, Little Blue, Greenbacked and Yellowcrowned Night Herons, and Common Moorhen** are examples of wandering marshbirds, while later shorebirds have included **Willet, Longbilled Dowitcher and Western Sandpiper**. The only regular October landbirds are those that habitually leave late like **Yellowbilled and Blackbilled Cuckoos, Redheaded Woodpecker, Eastern Kingbird, Water Pipit, Northern Shrike** and a selection of boreal thrushes, warblers, blackbirds and sparrows. **Warbling Vireo and Indigo Bunting** are regular, while some of the rarest vagrants have included **Gray Kingbird, Whiteeyed Vireo, Yellowthroated and Hooded Warblers, Blackheaded Grosbeak and Goldencrowned Sparrow. Bohemian Waxwing** sometimes arrive in early November, by which time the blackbird flocks are beginning to thin out in anticipation of winter.

Bibliography

Books (Field and Identification Guides/Books of Local Interest)

Baker, Ross H., *Reflections of a Bird Watcher*, Lancelot Press 1979

Boyer, George F., *Birds of the Nova Scotia — New Brunswick Border Region*, Canadian Wildlife Service 1972

Bruun & Singer, *Larousse Guide to Birds of Britain and Europe*, Larousse & Co. Inc. 1978

Bull & Farrand, *Audubon Society Field Guide to North American Birds: Eastern Region*, Alfred A. Knopf/Random House of Canada Ltd. 1977

Farrand, John Jr., *The Audubon Society Master Guide to Birding* (three volumes), Alfred A. Knopf/Random House of Canada Ltd. 1983

Finlay, J.C., *A Bird-Finding Guide to Canada*, Hurtig Publishers Ltd. 1984

Godfrey, Earl, *The Birds of Canada*, National Museums of Canada 1986

Grant, P.J., *Gulls*, Buteo Books 1982

Harrison, Peter, *Seabirds*, Croom Helm Ltd./ A.H. & A.W. Reed Ltd. 1983

Heinzel, Fitter, Parslow, *Birds of Britain and Europe with North Africa and the Middle East*, Collins 1977

National Geographic Society, *Field Guide to the Birds of North America*, National Geographic Society 1987

Peterson, Roger T., *A Field Guide to the Birds East of the Rockies*, Houghton Mifflin Company 1980

Rickert, Jon E. Sr., *A Guide to North American Bird Clubs*, Avian Publications 1978

Robbins, Bruun, Zim, Singer, *Birds of North America*, Golden Press 1983

Sharrock, J.T.R., *Frontiers of Bird Identification*, MacMillan Journals 1980

Stephenson, Marylee, *Canada's National Parks*, Prentice-Hall Canada, Inc. 1983

Tufts, Robie W., *Birds and Their Ways*, Lancelot Press 1985

Tufts, Robie W., *Birds of Nova Scotia*, Nimbus Publishing/NS Museum 1986

Booklets (Local Sites Only)

Dobson, Phyllis, *Finding Birds in Nova Scotia*, Nova Scotia Bird Society 1983

Tingley, Stuart, *Amherst Point Migratory Bird Sancutary*, Canadian Wildlife Service 1981

Magazines and Journals (National and Local)

American Birding Association, *Birding*, bimonthly USA

Bennett, Gerry, *Birdfinding in Canada*, bimonthly CAN

Canadian Nature Federation, *Seasons*, quarterly CAN

National Audubon Society, *American Birds*, bimonthly USA

Nova Scotia Bird Society, *Nova Scotia Birds*, quarterly NS

Checklists (International, National, Provincial and Local)

Barber Region, Nova Scotia-New Brunswick, *Checklist of Birds, Canadian Wildlife Service 1974*

British Trust for Ornithology, *List of the Birds of the Western Palearchic*, British Trust for Ornithology

Cape Breton Highlands, *Check List of Birds*, Parks Canada 1974

Chignecto National Wildlife Area (Amherst Point/Lusby), *Check-list of Birds*, Canadian Wildlife Service 1981

Kejimkujik National Park, *Birds of Kejimkujik*, Parks Canada 1985

Nova Scotia, *Check List*, Nova Scotia Bird Society

Tintamarre National Wildlife Area, *Check-list of Birds*, Canadian Wildlife Service 1980

Provincial Natural History Society

Nova Scotia Bird Society, c/o Nova Scotia Museum, 1747 Summer Street, Halifax, Nova Scotia, Canada B3H 3A6

Index to Sites

Not all locations mentioned in the site guide are indexed, only those that have reported enough times in local publications to suggest a visit is warranted. Some indexed locations include a number of recommended sites.